AFTERLIFE

life beyond death
for the departed and
new life for the grieving

david peters
with greta peters

AFTERLIFE

ISBN: 978-0-473-35324-7

Editor: Pene Ashby
McLaren Brown Media
(A division of McLaren Brown Publishing Ltd – since 1985)
mclarenbrownmedia.com

Printed and bound by CPI Group (UK) Ltd, Croydon, CR0 4YY
Published by SpiritLife Ministries.
www.spiritlife.org.nz

DEDICATION

To Jane and Ron

You ran well and lived lives that honoured your Lord. Now, from your vantage point of the great cloud of witnesses in heaven, you observe Greta's and my journey. One day we will join you, but now we pray we will run a good race for our Lord, as you did. Thank you for your love.
This is for you.

WHAT OTHERS ARE SAYING

David is one of the most solid, anointed prophetic teachers I know. In this book, he and his wife Greta lay out a sound biblical understanding on life after death and what God has promised for believers. They have walked the journey that no married person ever wants to face – the loss of a spouse. Afterlife made me weep for their journey and laugh with joy at the display of God's goodness as they walked through grief into wholeness again. This book is a must for anyone who has recently lost a loved one and gives both in-depth understanding and hope that God has provided the way to a glorious eternity.

– Lynley Allan, Pastor, Catch the Fire, Auckland, NZ

In their latest book, David and Greta Peters remind us of the reality of eternity, something that we need in an increasingly uncertain world. Laying a biblical foundation, and drawing on their own experience, they help us to see the profound importance of heaven and the eternal realm, not just as something in the distant future, but as a reality now. Interweaving biblical teaching with their own life stories, they also testify to how God comforts us in times of grief. For many Christians, especially those in the charismatic world, sudden tragedy or the healing that never comes in this life can become a serious blow to faith. David and Greta's confession that "God is good", even in their time of loss and sadness, combined with an eternal hope that goes beyond the pain and disappointment of this life, shows us how faith can prevail even in the greatest of storms.

– James Glass, Senior Pastor, Glasgow Elim Church; National Leadership Team, Elim Pentecostal Churches, UK

Afterlife begins with an engaging story of life, love and loss, then continues to discuss grief, gratitude and God. Anyone cannot help but empathise with David and Greta's story. Non-Christians could gain much by reading this as it opens a dimension of life they will not encounter in the world. David goes on to on address topics concerning life beyond death that puzzle many people. Each topic is addressed positively with a sound biblical basis and should fill every Christian with hope. More than that: it should convince readers who are not yet Christians to receive the salvation of Jesus Christ and his gift of eternal life. Many other books deal with just a few of the issues of the afterlife, rather than all of them as this book so ably does.

– R Errol Francis, author of "Lord Jesus Revive Us and Return to Us", Auckland, NZ

Afterlife addresses one of the universal questions of humanity: "What happens to us after we die?" This subject has been rife with misconceptions, misunderstandings and has fuelled much debate. David's timely book dispels some of the myths. It blends personal experience, prophetic insight and sound theology in a way that comforts, encourages and challenges. For those unsure or fearful of the future, Afterlife inspires hope and confidence. And for all of us it ignites a fresh passion for intimacy with God and a deeper concern for those not yet in His kingdom.

– Paul Bennetts, Founding Pastor, Life Church, Christchurch, NZ

This is a powerful, gritty, moving and encouraging message of finding comfort in the darkest storm and breaking through into the hope of a new day afterwards. David and Greta's story is of a couple who walked through the valley of the shadow of death and out into recovery and restoration afterwards.

– Norm McLeod, Senior Pastor, House of Breakthrough, Gisborne, NZ

CONTENTS

FOREWORD

For many people, one of life's biggest and most intriguing questions is, "What happens after we die?" In this book, my good friend David Peters who, along with his wife, Greta, is a highly valued prophet and partner of Church Unlimited, tackles this issue head-on with honesty and admirable courage, as he explores topics such as death, grief, healing, judgment, heaven and hell. These can be difficult subjects, but I would consider this biblical, beautifully written and compelling book absolutely vital reading.

A number of years ago my wife and I were with a group of family members and close friends of a young wife and mother, who was desperately sick from a lifelong congenital condition. She was, in fact, unconscious, and on life support in the Critical Care Unit. The head doctor gathered us around the table in a conference room to update us on the patient's condition when a nurse burst into the room to tell us the patient had taken a turn for the worse. We rushed to the bedside but it was too late. I will never forget that woman's lovely mother, tears streaming down her face, saying over and over, "Thank you God for such a wonderful daughter."

Such an amazing and godly attitude brought to mind Job's words when he faced the unbelievable loss of everything he owned and, worst of all, his ten children: "The Lord gave, and the Lord has taken away; Blessed be the name of the Lord." (Job 1:21 NKJV)

I first met David when he spoke at one of our men's breakfasts. He shared the very moving story of the death of his first wife, Jane. Jane suffered from multiple sclerosis, but through all the years of this progressive and debilitating condition David never gave up praying and believing for her healing. Sadly, that did not happen. When Jane passed away, he displayed that same godly attitude as Job; he actually repeated Job's words, "The Lord gave, and the Lord has taken away; Blessed be the name of the Lord." At that time, he determined he would not allow himself to become offended with God because Jane hadn't been healed. To me that encapsulates the stature of the man.

Isaiah 45:3 (NKJV) says, "I will give you the treasures of darkness And hidden riches of secret places." We know that beautiful and valuable gems – diamonds, sapphires, emeralds and so on – are formed by immense pressure over a long period of time; then they have to be painstakingly dug out of deep and dark places in the earth. Well, the same can be true in the spiritual realm, and individually David and Greta have certainly experienced some great pressure and deep, dark places. But they have responded admirably to God and have come out the other side better, not bitter. This book will inspire you to do likewise, as you face your own seasons of darkness; which are not about being singled out for the bad stuff, but simply part and parcel of life on this fallen and sin-sick planet.

In this book, David opens his treasure trove, as it were, and allows us to look inside and see the incredible richness of the great depth of understanding, insight and revelation in God's word that he has gained from his experiences and study around sickness, death, and what happens to people after they die. Some of the precious truths contained within the following pages include both David and Greta's accounts of the grief they suffered following the loss of their much-loved spouses. Yes, it's real and it's raw, but both resound with the great hope and the reality of the God of all comfort, who was most definitely there for them in their time of need.

You will see how the story of the Children of Israel encountering the bitter waters of Marah is a timeless treasure, and how God, through the cross of Christ, can make our bitter waters sweet, and turn our losses to gain. And who doesn't love a love story? You will be blessed as you read how God brought David and Greta together.

Chapter eight is a powerful study on healing. I have a friend in ministry who had a kind of crisis when God didn't answer his prayers while he was on a mission trip. His response was to affirm, "I don't always see what I believe but I still believe what I believe." Isn't that the truth?

David does a great job of fearlessly and honestly facing the mystery of unanswered prayer for healing. He also explores the origins of sickness and disease, hindrances to healing, and how to pray for healing. Jane was not healed in this life, but now David and Greta have a powerful healing ministry and further, are training the body of Christ around the world to exercise this ministry, along with other gifts of the Holy Spirit.

Part two moves on to life beyond death for those who have passed on. David quotes Ecclesiastes 3:11 (NIV), which says, "He (God) has also set eternity in the human heart." Little wonder then, that the question regarding what happens after death has concerned and fascinated humankind since the beginning of time.

We read about judgment, hell, heaven, and what kind of heavenly bodies we will have. As David points out, our doctrine comes from the Bible. I believe his teaching on these realities will answer many questions both believers and non-believers may have on various issues. I was grateful to see him clearly address three of the main false ideas about hell, especially the pernicious theory of annihilation, which so many Christians embrace today.

What a joy to read the truths about heaven, and these truths are wonderfully enhanced by visions God has enabled David, Greta, and others, to experience. I believe it is vital that we have a strong (biblical) concept of eternity, including the truth about heavenly rewards, in order to be fully motivated to live holy and godly lives. Afterlife contains some powerful teaching on the kind of life God rewards.

In this brilliant book, David does not shy away from any aspect of truth but, despite the solemnity of the subject matter, it is full of life and hope. I would highly recommend it for all, Christian and non-Christian alike.

– Tak Bhana, Senior Pastor, Church Unlimited, New Zealand.

INTRODUCTION

The thought of writing this book occurred to me a number of years ago when I taught a series of messages on life beyond death. It included such topics as what happens when we die, the Day of Judgment, the body we will have in the resurrection, the new earth and heavens God will create one day, and so forth. However, I felt unable to write it. Fearing that it would be merely a clinical teaching book, lacking any personal element that people could relate to, I dismissed the idea.

All this changed dramatically in November 2007 when Jane, my wife of many years, passed away suddenly, taken finally by the multiple sclerosis she had battled so bravely against for more than three decades. Now eternity became vividly real, its doorway open before me. Instantly this topic leapt from the pages of theoretical doctrine to become a poignantly real and emotive subject.

In my first book, *Hope – Finding the Doorway to a Better Future*, I wrote extensively about Jane's and my earlier journey through disease and adversity to a place of robust hope, unwavering confidence in the goodness of God, and a strong expectation that God would heal Jane miraculously. When Jane died, that expectation lay shattered.

It provoked me to ask some deep questions.

How can we make sense of unfulfilled hopes and seemingly unanswered prayers? How can a person navigate through the crippling darkness of grief that envelopes them when a loved one is lost? Is there life for the living beyond bereavement? And what of the dead? Is there life beyond death for them? What is it like? Are heaven and hell real places? Is there an afterlife? It is vital that we find answers to these all-important questions.

Shortly after Jane died, the teenage daughter of my gym instructor lost her grandmother. This young woman was desolate with grief over her death, compounded by the knowledge that she had no idea where her beloved grandmother was now. Without faith in God, death was a numbing loss to her, and she did not know what, if anything, lay on the other side of it. She had no hope.

Millions today live without hope in an afterlife, and as well as making it harder to recover from grief, it causes them to live only for present pleasure, instead of devoting their lives to God and the rewards for faithful living he promises to give in eternity.

Are there answers to the questions we have posed? The response is a resounding, "Yes!" From a careful study of the scriptures, and visions of heaven the Holy Spirit has graciously given to others and me, I have attempted, through this book, to bring light to those suffering from the devastating loss of a loved one, or any other kind of serious loss. I also want to instil a sense of divine purpose in those who desire to live responsibly in this life because of the glories they glimpse of the next.

Over time, God healed my grief and brought my new wife Greta into my life. Her husband Ron passed away a few months after Jane. What God taught us both about his power to heal grieving hearts and give fresh meaning to our lives, as well as the afterlife beyond death, are found in the pages that follow. There truly is hope for the living and for the dead.

PART 1

LIFE BEYOND DEATH FOR THE LIVING

chapter one

ETERNITY CALLS

When Jane and I married we were young and deeply in love. Five years before, doctors had diagnosed that she had multiple sclerosis (MS). They warned that this degenerative disease of the nervous system would slowly, but inevitably, confine Jane to a wheelchair. She was in remission at the time we married, but over the following years, developed a chronic progressive form of the disease, and their prediction came true. By 1986, she began to use a wheelchair, and five years later could no longer stand, hold anything, or care for herself. Resigning from my leadership role in a large city church, I became her caregiver for the next sixteen years.

Though we fought in prayer and faith for divine healing, Jane's health continued to worsen, so that by 2007, the disease had made both swallowing and breathing difficult. Frequent lung infections resulted and on the morning of November 5th, I woke to hear Jane wheezing and struggling for breath. Contacting her doctor, who prescribed antibiotics and promised to visit later in the day, I made Jane as comfortable as I could.

Then I began to fast and pray. If ever we needed a miracle, it was now.

After an impassioned time of prayer that morning, I went to pray again in the afternoon. As I began, the Holy Spirit interrupted me: "Are you willing to let Jane go?" Realising the serious consequences of my response, I pondered this question for some time. Finally, I replied, "Yes, Lord," hoping that this was merely a test of my will and that healing would still result. A few minutes later, the phone rang. It was a close friend.
"How's Jane?" he asked.
"Not good," I replied.
"I have been praying and I feel that the Lord is asking you to surrender her into his hands and trust him for the outcome."

Again, I agonised over this. We had fought so hard for healing for more than twenty years. That struggle had defined my life and relationship with the Lord. Now I was being asked to let it go. *The Lord is worthy of my full trust*, I thought, even if the outcome is not as I desire it. Realising that it was out of my hands, once more I prayed and said, "I give her into your hands Lord." God had graciously prepared me for what would happen next.

A few hours later, Jane suddenly stopped breathing (the autopsy would later show she had developed pneumonia). A neighbour tried to resuscitate her while I dialled emergency services. Arriving quickly, the paramedics worked feverishly to try to revive her. After what seemed an eternity, the head medic came and said, "I am very sorry, Mr Peters. We did everything we could, but she is gone." His words pierced my heart, and I sobbed deeply.

Composing myself, I walked slowly to the bedroom where her still warm body lay. After saying tearful goodbyes to my wife of thirty years, I put my hand on her head and said, "The Lord gave, and the Lord has taken away; Blessed be the name of the Lord."[1] Refusing to be offended because God had not healed her, I chose to bow to his sovereignty. The apostle Paul writes, "Now [in this life] I know in part; but then [in eternity] I shall know fully."[2] The gap between knowing in part and knowing in full is called mystery. I didn't have all the answers but was prepared to live with that mystery, despite the devastating loss. The second decision I made was to not retreat from belief in divine healing. In fact, I vowed to not only keep praying for the sick but also to train others to do it.

An Exploding Sky

Later that night, after family and friends had said their farewells, we carried Jane's body out to the waiting hearse. November 5th is Guy Fawkes Day in New Zealand, commemorating the foiling of a plot to blow up British Parliament on that day in 1605, and is celebrated with fireworks. As if waiting for our procession, the dark, clear sky erupted with skyrockets, filling the air with brilliant bursts of red, yellow, blue, white, and green as far as the eye could see. It seemed that heaven was celebrating her homecoming after a life so well lived. Another neighbour, who is not a churchgoer, commented on how unusual it was. November 5th was also Lynne's birthday. Lynne, Jane's sister, had died at age twenty from lung cancer some forty years before.

---

1 Job 1:21(NKJV)

2 1 Corinthians 13: 12 (NIV)

No doubt as a Christian she would be in heaven's welcoming party, as Jane reached home.

Afterwards, I took our sons Joseph, Adam, and Tim aside to talk with them. Like me, they were grieving their mother's death deeply. "Boys," I said, "Mum and I prayed confidently for a miracle of healing, and I want to ask your forgiveness if, in doing that, I have caused you to become disappointed or even angry at God."

"Dad," they replied, "we are glad that you believed for Mum to be healed."

Too many times I have seen parents declare that God will do certain things, only for their children to become extremely hurt and turn away from God when they don't happen. The offence only deepens when simplistic explanations are given. It is important to be honest, humble, and to try not to give answers if there are none. We attempt to give explanations to ease the pain and end up creating more pain.

For example, trying to explain to a young child why his or her parent has died, by saying that God wanted Mummy (or Daddy) in heaven more than here on earth, makes God look mean and may set up resentment in the child's mind. "We try to give explanations when God is giving none," warns Bill Johnson.[3]

Rick Warren, author of *The Purpose Driven Life*, suffered a devastating loss when his son committed suicide after years of battling mental illness and loss of hope.

---

[3] Senior Pastor, Bethel Church, Redding, California

In his first sermon some months after his son's death, he stated, "I would rather walk with God and not have my question answered than have my question answered, but not walk with God."

Climbing into bed that night, I cried out to Jesus to help me in my distress, and after some time managed to fall asleep, exhausted from the events of the day. This will sound strange, but two to three times in the night, I heard an audible, "Wheee!" I could imagine Jane's elation in heaven, free from confinement at last. When I awoke the next morning, I took my Bible, and turned to 2 Chronicles chapter 36, as directed by my reading guide. As I read, verse 21 arrested me, "The land enjoyed its Sabbath rests; all the time of its desolation it rested." These words were revelation to me: Jane now enjoyed rest from the weary decades of battling MS, and God would give me rest from the fatigue of sixteen years of caregiving. Furthermore, the way through the desolation of loss, was not to strive, but rest in his love.

Victorious Funeral

A few days later, more than a thousand people attended Jane's funeral, which was a triumphant time of celebration. "We do not want you to be uninformed about those who sleep in death," writes the apostle Paul, "so that you do not grieve like the rest of mankind, who have no hope."[4]

Believers in Christ, although they grieve the loss of a loved one, know it is only a temporary separation, and Paul adds,

---

4 1 Thessalonians 4:13 (NIV)

"For since we believe that Jesus died and was raised to life again, we also believe that when Jesus returns, God will bring back with him the believers who have died."[5]

The funeral's theme, *A Lifetime of Smiles*, reflected the fact that Jane had smiled her way through intense adversity for many years. I purposely chose as one of the songs *Blessed Be Your Name* [6] as it contained the following poignant words:

Every blessing you pour out, I'll turn back to praise,
And when the darkness closes in, Lord still I will say,
Blessed be the name of the Lord,
blessed be the name of the Lord.
You give and take away; you give and take away,
My heart will choose to say, Lord blessed be your name.

Later, close family and friends attended the graveside ceremony with me. As I scanned the nearby graves, I observed that some had become shrines with photos, memorabilia and other items adorning the plots. *Many sadly have only the grave and no hope beyond that,* I reflected to myself. I knew unshakably that Jane was alive in heaven.

Nevertheless, the tearful last goodbyes, as the casket was lowered into the ground, still lent such an air of finality. A friend had composed a song especially for this occasion, and, as he sang the chorus, "Free at last, dancing in heaven; Free at last, perfect healing,"[7] my mind flashed back to the night I had heard that

---

5 1 Thessalonians 4:14

6 *Blessed Be Your Name*, Matt Redman, ©2002, ThankYou Music/ Kingsway Music. Abbreviated lyrics

7 David Lyle Morris, *Jane's Song*, ©2007, Tevita Music

strange, audible sound in my bedroom. Perhaps that is what Jane had been doing in heaven – dancing.

The next day, a walk downtown to purchase some supplies felt so surreal. People scurried from shop to shop, oblivious to the fact that I had lost my wife. Didn't they know? Couldn't they see? For them, life continued as normal but for me, it was very different. Over the next week, a thick darkness enveloped me. People said to me repeatedly that Jane was now completely healed in heaven but it was cold comfort. I felt desolate, overcome with loss and grief, and angry that I was so disconnected from my wife. Jane was in Paradise having a wonderful time and I was on earth where life was unbearably painful. At my darkest moment exactly a week after the funeral, I cried out to God, "Lord, I don't know how to get through this. You have got to help me." A few minutes later, the beeping of my mobile phone interrupted my thoughts.

It was a text message from a friend. His wife had had an operation that day. The text simply said that she was fine and had seen Jane. Mystified, I phoned him and discovered that his wife claimed that, while under the anesthetic, her spirit went to heaven. She later told me: "I expected to see someone important like Jesus, or Paul, or Moses, but I saw Jane. She was smiling, standing and praising God. She walked towards me and said, 'I'm home!' It was like seeing an old friend or family member you'd known all your life, even though I had only known her casually over the last few years. It was as if we were sisters. It was a hugely encouraging impression of how relationships are in heaven."

That was a turning point for me. The doorway of hope in my intense valley of trouble creaked open a little, and some light shone through. Over the next few weeks, scriptures I had read many times now came alive with new meaning. "For to me, to live is Christ and to die is gain," writes the apostle Paul. "I am torn between the two: I desire to depart and be with Christ, which is better by far; but it is more necessary for you that I remain in the body."[8]

Furthermore, the Bible says that when you come to heaven, you not only come to God himself and myriads of angels, but also "to the spirits of the righteous in heaven who have now been made perfect."[9]

I concluded that, in death, Jane had gained something far better, and was now a perfected spirit in heaven, awaiting her glorious new body at the resurrection of believers. She was in the very presence of God and singing again. That was even better than being healed on earth, as wonderful as that would have been. This comforted me, but grief is a strange thing: just when you think you are making progress, a photo, a memory or a possession of the loved one can trigger a slide into darkness again. Depression, loneliness, anger, guilt and pain may all result. For example, I felt relieved that I was no longer Jane's caregiver, but battled guilt for feeling that way. I felt happy to gather all Jane's disability equipment and see the truck take it away, but could not face touching her clothes in the wardrobe.

It was while watching a Disney animated movie, of all things, that further light came. In Meet the Robinsons[10] there is a phrase that recurs throughout the film: "Keep moving forward."

---

8 Philippians 1:21, 23-24 (NIV)

9 Hebrews 12:23

10 Meet the Robinsons, © Walt Disney Pictures, 2007

Apparently, this was the motto of Walt Disney himself. It is alright to grieve and to be patient with the process. Some days it will feel like three steps forward and two back. However, we must not become stuck in grief. Grief is a valley to pass through, not a canyon to camp in. When the patriarch Jacob lost his beloved wife Rachel on the way back to the Promised Land from Mesopotamia, the Bible records, "Rachel died and was buried on the way to Ephrath (that is, Bethlehem). Jacob set up a stone monument over Rachel's grave, and it can be seen there to this day. Then Jacob travelled on."[11]

Jacob, though grieving deeply, did not camp by the monument, but travelled on. In the same way, I had to move on, choosing to mourn less over what I had lost, and rejoice more over what Jane had gained. She had gained God's presence in death, and now I needed to gain Christ in life and journey through grief successfully. In the next chapter, we will explore how to do this.

---

11 Genesis 35:19-21

chapter two

GRIEF'S JOURNEY

Grief arrives unannounced and unwelcomed at the death of a loved one, or the loss of a treasured possession such as a relationship, career, health, or finance. In the case of marriage, the surviving spouse will often feel as if half their soul has been ripped out. I have navigated many valleys of trouble and difficulty in my lifetime, but there has been no darker or deeper valley than this one of grief and loss or, as the psalmist puts it, *the valley of the shadow of death.*[1]

The journey to wholeness again may take months or years and, sadly, some people never recover, grieving their entire lives. Because she constantly mourned the loss of her beloved Prince Albert in 1861, after twenty-one years of marriage, Queen Victoria wore black for the rest of her life. She died in 1901. In a recently discovered letter that she wrote some fifteen months after Albert's death, to 82-year-old Viscount Gough, one

---

1 Psalm 23:4 (NKJV)

of Britain's greatest military heroes of the nineteenth century, she sends her condolences on the death of his wife:

> The Queen has heard with much concern of the sad affliction that has befallen Lord Gough and is anxious to express personally her sincere sympathy to him. Irreparable as his loss is, how blessed to have lived together until the evening of their lives with the comfort and hope of the separation being a short one. To the poor Queen this blessing so needful to her has been denied, and she can only hope never to live to old age but be allowed to rejoin her beloved great and loyal husband before many years elapse.[2]

This longing to die, in order to be with the loved one, may be strong in the early days of grief. Separation feels unbearable and nothing seems to soothe the pain. This is normal. In fact, realising that the many different characteristics of grief are quite typical can be the key to journeying through it. These factors vary, but fall into four broad categories – feelings, physical sensations, behaviours and thoughts.[3]

---

2 www.dailymail.co.uk/news/article-2073792/Queen-Victorias-unbearable-grief-death-Prince-Albert.html, accessed 30/11/12

3 Adapted from *Understanding Grief and Loss* workbook, Blueprint Centre for Learning, 2007. Used by permission.

Feelings

- Sadness and depression
- Anger
- Emancipation
- Anxiety
- Loneliness
- Yearning for lost person/object
- Shock
- Guilt and self-reproach
- Relief
- Numbness
- Regret
- Helplessness

Physical Sensations

- Fatigue
- Breathlessness
- Tightness in the chest
- Hollowness in stomach
- Oversensitivity to noise
- Weakness in the muscles

Behaviours

- Disturbed sleep
- Loss of appetite
- Absent mindedness
- Dreams of the lost person/object
- Visiting places or carrying objects that remind of the lost person
- Crying
- Social withdrawal
- Treasuring the lost person's possessions
- Restless over-activity
- Avoiding reminders of the lost person/object

Thoughts

- Disbelief – it didn't happen
- Confusion
- Preoccupation with thoughts of the lost person/object
- 'I walk down the street and nothing seems real'
- 'I wish I was dead'
- A sense of presence of the lost person/object

The list is not exhaustive, and nor will one person necessarily experience all of these characteristics. Because some of the sensations suffered by a grieving person will be frightening, it can be helpful to know what is normal and usual. Grief can be successfully navigated with the help of caring friends and especially with Jesus' help, for he is well acquainted with it. Speaking of Jesus, the Bible records, "He was despised and rejected – a man of sorrows, acquainted with deepest grief."[4] As he prayed in the garden of Gethsemane the night before he was crucified, Jesus told his disciples, "My soul is crushed with grief to the point of death. Stay here and keep watch with me."[5]

The greatest loss in history occurred when the Father gave his son over to sin, to the cross, and to death. In that moment, a perfect relationship that stretched into eternity past, fractured, causing Jesus' anguished cry, "My God, my God, why have you forsaken me?"[6] Similarly, deep sorrow pierced the Father's heart in having to reject his son. Jesus' grief was so great that it killed him – his legs did not need to be broken to hasten death, like the two men crucified with him. God can comfort us because

---

4 Isaiah 53:3

5 Mark 14:34

6 Matthew 27:46 (NIV)

he has shared our pain. If we trust his goodness, and resist the temptation to be resentful that he did not intervene to prevent our loss, then we will know his supernatural comfort.

Some Good Advice

As the weeks stretched by after Jane's death, God continued to shine light into my pained soul. Though, in the first few months the journey was very up and down emotionally, it began to level out. I found it important to be around close friends and to talk about Jane, her death, heaven, and my feelings. A Christian counsellor advised, "Don't rush the process of grief. Allow time for rest and recovery and listen to your body: rest when it says rest and exercise when it says exercise. Keep talking things through, even if you repeat yourself. Your family and friends will understand. The pain you feel is a sign that you are fully alive." He also warned that grief lowers all defences and makes us vulnerable. Because we are so open to receive encouragement and comfort, we are as equally open to be hurt by negative and harmful comments, or fall into a premature relationship, and so must guard our hearts. Honesty with the Lord, and with close friends, is vital in this stage.

Many of the psalms in the Bible are the record of grieving people being extremely honest with their God. "O LORD, how long will you forget me?" wrote Israel's King David, "How long must I struggle with anguish in my soul, with sorrow in my heart every day? Turn and answer me, O LORD my God! Restore the sparkle to my eyes, or I will die." David finishes on a hopeful note however, when he writes, "But I trust in your unfailing love. I will rejoice because you have rescued me. I will sing to the LORD because he is good to me."[7] If we remind ourselves of God's deliverance and goodness in the past, like David, we will have hope for the future. *But I trust* are powerful words when navigating grief.

Another friend shared his wisdom after navigating great loss in his own life: "Get physically fit, as some people fall apart within two to three years of a grievous loss, and being well fit really helps." I made sure I continued my regime at the local gym and tried new physical activities such as mountain-biking.

Home did not help for as well as being a place to live, it was also a place of work. It was where I had cared for Jane. An office also occupied one of the rooms for me to work on ministry matters. It would have been better to work elsewhere and leave the house and all its reminders of Jane, but I had nowhere to go. It felt strange – the caregiving role had filled my days, and now I didn't know what to do. Who was I? I had been a caregiver, Jane's husband, and a part-time itinerant preacher. Those roles had defined me, but now the first two had gone, and the third was on hold. I was having an identity crisis. When I felt overcome, I escaped the house and walked. And as I walked, I talked. To God. About everything. It wasn't the type of intercessory prayer I had been so used to – it was more like chatting.

In fact, for weeks after losing Jane, I had been unable to pray earnestly about much at all. Her death seemed to have removed spiritual energy from me. But I could converse with God. And I could worship. Often, lying on my bed, I would listen to worship music – loving the Lord and letting him minister

---

7 Psalm 13: 1-3, 5-6

his love and comfort to me. I have no doubt that this intimacy with him accelerated my recovery. In the midst of these worship or 'soaking' times I heard God's voice. He whispered that my identity was not in what I did but in who I was. I was his son and he was my Father. And he gave me revelation from the scriptures. As I read the Bible each day, I found it comforted my soul, giving me hope that all would end well.

For example, I was troubled occasionally by flashbacks to Jane's death, asking myself guiltily whether I could have done more to prevent it. Then I read in the book of Job, "In his hand is the life of every creature and the breath of all mankind."[8] Our life breath is ultimately in God's hands, and not anyone else's. Isaiah the prophet commented, "Good people pass away; the godly often die before their time. But no one seems to care or wonder why. No one seems to understand that God is protecting them from the evil to come."[9]

As I meditated on these scriptures, I concluded that MS, though taking Jane's life, had not won. Its evil grip had affected her life for many years, but now she was free in heaven, far beyond her suffering on earth, and spared from worse to come. I accepted God's decision to promote her to heaven, rather than heal her on earth, for he sees far more clearly than we do.

Seeing Clearly

I noted that the song *Blessed be Your Name* sung at Jane's funeral, was based on Job's statement, "Naked I came from

---

8 Job 12:10 (NIV)
9 Isaiah 57:1

my mother's womb, and naked shall I return: The LORD gave and the LORD has taken away; blessed be the name of the LORD."[10] The capitalised LORD in this verse is a substitute for the Hebrew name YHWH (or Yahweh) meaning I AM, the eternally unchanging, faithful, and loving one, who cannot deny his nature. We easily believe this when God gives, but find it harder to believe when he appears to take away. It looks and feels like subtraction and loss. We need to get God's perspective. It changes everything. He sees into eternity, we focus on the finite. He knows the end of the story, we don't. And the end of a matter is better than the beginning.

An unusual experience vividly illustrated this to me one day when I ran some errands to the local shops and then finished up at the church office. As I walked into reception, the church administrator asked, "What is wrong with your eye?" Taking my glasses off, I discovered that one of the lenses had fallen out. Because they were transition lenses that darkened in sunlight, one eye was dark and the other normal where the missing lens had been. Absent-mindedness is supposedly a part of grief, so I have no idea at what stage the lens dropped out or how long I had been walking around town like that. New glasses with more powerful lenses resulted, and I was astonished at how much more clearly I could see. This was such a strange event that I sensed there could be a message in it, so I asked the Lord about it. I sensed the Holy Spirit reply, "You lost one lens but gained two better ones. In this season of loss, you will see much more clearly than ever before." This would prove to be very true in the coming months.

---

10 Job 1:21 (RSV)

Keeping Proper Perspective

In the book of Ruth, we read the moving story of Naomi (whose name means Pleasant) and her family who lived in Bethlehem (which means House of Bread). When famine came and there was no longer bread in the house of bread, Naomi, her husband and two sons moved to the land of Moab. There the young men married Moabite women. As the years rolled by, Naomi's husband and two sons all died. Later, when she heard that the famine was over, Naomi decided to return to Bethlehem. She encouraged her daughters-in-law to stay in Moab but Ruth could not be persuaded, and accompanied her mother-in-law on the journey. Excited by their arrival, the townsfolk welcomed Naomi home.

"Don't call me Naomi," she responded. "Instead, call me Mara, (which means *Bitter*) for the Almighty has made life very bitter for me. I went away full, but the LORD has brought me home empty. Why call me Naomi when the LORD has caused me to suffer and the Almighty has sent such tragedy upon me?"[11]

Naomi's theology was very negative. She blamed God for her losses. When people grieve, they may say things that are negative or incorrect. It is their pain talking. It is not wise to correct their faulty view at this time. The sickroom is not the place to debate theology. Rather, love them, pray for them, and be patient. Over time, the Lord will give them proper perspective, just as I received new glasses to see more clearly.

Things ended well for Naomi. Ruth married Naomi's wealthy relative Boaz, and soon baby Obed was born. "Praise the LORD,"

---

11 Ruth 1:20, 21

exclaimed the town's women excitedly, "who has now provided a redeemer for your family! May this child be famous in Israel. May he restore your youth and care for you in your old age. For he is the son of your daughter-in-law who loves you and has been better to you than seven sons! Naomi took the baby and cuddled him to her breast. And she cared for him as if he were her own."[12]

Obed would one day become the grandfather of David, one of Israel's greatest kings, and an ancestor of Jesus. God knows how to redeem loss and turn it to gain. "God will shatter lesser dreams in our lives," writes Dr Larry Crabb, "in order to give us greater dreams, especially the desire to know him better."[13]

These truths gave me strong hope for the future and the tide of my grief began to turn. And when the Holy Spirit started to give me visions of heaven, it receded even further.

---

12 Ruth 4:14-16

13 *Shattered Dreams*, Colorado Springs, Waterbrook Press, 2001.

chapter three

HEAVEN IS OPEN

It was a Monday; exactly three weeks after Jane had passed away. The evening before, I had attended a meeting where John and Carol Arnott, leaders of the Toronto outpouring of the mid-nineties, were speaking. As Carol prayed for me, the power of the Holy Spirit came upon me so strongly that I fell over and remained on the floor for nearly an hour or so, soaking in God's love. The next morning, I met with a pastor who described some visions of heaven the Lord had given him, which stirred faith within me. Providentially, this combination of anointing and faith was about to open a door into a realm that I had never entered before. That afternoon, I drove to the beach to spend time with the Lord. As I relaxed in my car seat, I closed my eyes, and suddenly began to see into another world. Although I could hear the waves gently lapping the sand and shrieks of delight from children playing in the water, my attention was riveted on the vision[1] unfolding in my mind.

Jesus, clothed in a pure white robe radiant with light, stood beside a sparkling, crystal-clear pool of water. Encircled by exquisite plants, it was fed by a waterfall that cascaded into it from high above. Jesus' warm smile invited me to approach. I walked to him, then we ascended to the top of the waterfall, and stood on the edge of a vast plain that looked yellow, as if drought-affected, which seemed odd to me. In the distance stood a magnificent, golden city with high walls and tall towers reaching into the heavens. From it a river flowed, which wound its way across the plain towards us, it being the source of the waterfall. As we walked besides the river towards the city, I looked down and noticed that the grass was actually brilliant green under my feet. The glow of the city gave it a golden hue when looked at from a distance. Everything seemed bathed in the glory emanating from the city.

Entering a gate, we walked through the streets, which bustled with people. Individuals kept saying, "Hello David!" and appeared to know me, but I did not know them. As Jesus led me further into the city, I noticed five people standing together in the distance. As we drew near, I recognised my mother and father, Jane's father and older sister Lynne (both of whom had pre-deceased her), and Jane herself. Clothed in white, she looked

1 Visions that others or I have had are a common occurrence in this book. Some Christians may struggle with such spiritual experiences, yet the Bible openly declares that, in the last days, (the time between Christ's first and second comings) the Lord will pour out his Spirit on all flesh and people will have visions, dreams, and will prophesy. See Acts 2:17-18. Thus, God means visions to be a normal part of the Christian life and, as long as we test them against scripture, we can accept them as helpful prophetic encouragement.

young and beautiful. It was a joyful meeting and I sensed such deep love in them for me. They smiled at me but did not speak. Perhaps they did not want to draw my focus and attention away from Jesus onto them. Jesus beckoned me to walk on, and as we did so, asked, "What would you like to see next?" Instantly I responded, "The Father!" Jesus smiled and seemed pleased that I had requested that. He then took me to the throne of God in the centre of the city. Before me was a huge orb of dazzling light, but within it, I could make out a figure sitting on a throne. As I continued to gaze at it, a thick, laser-like shaft of light shone out and penetrated my heart. As God poured his concentrated love into me, a peace flooded my soul. Then the vision ended.

This truly profound experience began to accelerate my healing from the grief of losing Jane. However, I knew it would be a mistake to form theology or doctrine from a vision. It drove me to the Bible to investigate further, and to my amazement, I discovered that heaven is not closed but open. "But if you don't believe me when I tell you about earthly things," warned Jesus, "how can you possibly believe if I tell you about heavenly things?"[2] Jesus desires to tell us of this heavenly world!

Heaven is Real

Heaven is a real place. Spectacular forests and paths, beautiful lakes and waterfalls, green fields and parks, and luscious gardens form part of its glory. A great river flows through a magnificent city filled with wide streets and grand mansions. Angels and saints live there and God himself. There is no aging, death, sickness, lack, or suffering. And heaven is open, accessible,

---

2 John 3:12

nearer than we think. Death is not the only gateway to it. Something is happening today. The veil between heaven and earth is getting very thin. Many report angelic visitations in unprecedented frequency, while others report visions of, or visitations to, heaven. Books on this are bestsellers.[3]

The book of Genesis records one of the earliest mentions of heaven in the Bible. Having left his home due to conflict with his brother Esau, the patriarch Jacob travelled to Mesopotamia to seek refuge with his relatives. On the way, he stopped the night at Bethel to rest. "As he slept," the Bible records, "he dreamed of a stairway that reached from the earth up to heaven. And he saw the angels of God going up and down the stairway."[4] Frightened, Jacob exclaimed, "What an awesome place this is! It is none other than the house of God, the very gateway to heaven!"[5]

The words *stairway* and *gateway* suggest that heaven interacts with earth and is not inaccessible until after death. Indeed, Jesus encouraged us to pray that the Kingdom of heaven would come to earth – not only when he returns, but now, so that its influence would fill the earth. As Bill Johnson points out, "Our destiny is heaven; our assignment is to bring heaven to earth." But, how can we bring heaven to earth if we have no idea what heaven is like, or what heaven is doing?

---

3 An erroneous concept of where heaven is has crept into Christendom: that heaven is very far away, perhaps amongst or beyond the stars. Therefore, it is unreachable by any means other than death. However, both scripture and Jesus made heaven seem very close. Science also proposes that the material and spiritual realms can exist closely together but be simply out of phase.

4 Genesis 28:12

5 Genesis 28:17

Jesus claimed that heaven could be opened. "Truly, truly," he said, echoing Jacob's discovery, "you will see heaven opened, and the angels of God ascending and descending upon the Son of man."[6] His entire ministry was an interaction of heaven with earth. Heaven opens where there is fervent prayer and expectation.[7] God is opening the heavens to many today, because of the unprecedented prayer that is taking place globally. This is a controversial thought to numbers of sincere believers who criticise such things as being an attempt to talk to the dead, a New Age teaching, or worse, 'of the devil'. This is nothing new.

Decades ago, controversy raged around the baptism of the Holy Spirit and speaking in tongues, truths that many in mainstream Christianity now accept happily. One thing is important however – we should not use experiences, no matter how powerful or real, to create doctrine. Only scripture can teach us sound beliefs, so it is to the Bible that we must turn, for evidence of heaven interacting with earth.

Visions of Heaven in Scripture

"In my thirtieth year," writes the prophet Ezekiel, "the heavens were opened and I saw visions of God."[8] Ezekiel goes on to describe visions of God and his throne that are some of the most extraordinary in the Bible, including seeing cherubim (angels associated with the presence and glory of God), one of the most unusual classes of angels in heaven. Isaiah was another prophet who had visions of heaven. "It was in the year

---

6 John 1:51
7 See Luke 3:21
8 Ezekiel 1:1 (NIV)

King Uzziah died that I saw the Lord," he says. "He was sitting on a lofty throne, and the train of his robe filled the Temple. Attending him were mighty seraphim, each having six wings."[9] (Seraphim are angels associated with the holiness of God and worship of him.)

Centuries before, the prophet Micaiah described to evil King Ahab of Israel the following vision, "I saw the LORD sitting on his throne with all the armies of heaven around him, on his right and on his left. And the LORD said, 'Who can entice Ahab to go into battle against Ramoth-gilead so he can be killed?'"[10] Micaiah apparently saw into the war council of God's throne room, where heavenly strategies were being decided.

In the New Testament, Stephen, the first martyr of the Christian church, whilst being interrogated by the Jewish High Council, saw into heaven: "But Stephen, full of the Holy Spirit, gazed steadily into heaven and saw the glory of God, and he saw Jesus standing in the place of honour at God's right hand. And he told them, 'Look, I see the heavens opened and the Son of Man standing in the place of honour at God's right hand!'"[11] A few years later, the apostle Peter, while praying, saw heaven opened and something like a large sheet full of living creatures being let down to earth by its four corners.[12]

This would later prove to be an insightful vision that would help the early Jewish Christians to accept Gentile believers into their fold.

---

9 Isaiah 6:1-2
10 1 Kings 22:19-20
11 Acts 7:55-56
12 See Acts 10:11 (NIV)

In such visions, the Holy Spirit peels open the invisible, spiritual realm so that we may see into it, with either our actual eyes (an open vision) or our mind's eye (a closed vision). Just because it is invisible does not mean that it is not real. These visions have several purposes: to draw us nearer to God, bring revelation of God's plans, and inspire us to have hope for the afterlife. Visions of heaven are very powerful. Visitations into heaven are even more so.

Visitations into Heaven in Scripture

"I was caught up to the third heaven[13] fourteen years ago," claimed the apostle Paul. "Whether I was in my body or out of my body, I don't know – only God knows. But I do know that I was caught up to paradise and heard things so astounding that they cannot be expressed in words ..."[14] Paul found this experience so overwhelming that he was unsure whether the Lord had taken him bodily into heaven (as happened to Enoch and Elijah, except that they did not return to earth[15]) or whether his spirit left his body temporarily and entered that realm. Apparently, both are possible. This is quite different to a vision, where the body and spirit of a person remains on earth, but God opens his or her senses to see into heaven. In a visitation, the person is actually in heaven, either in body (rarer) or in spirit (more common).

---

13 Most Bible scholars say that the first heaven is the sky above the earth, the second heaven is space and the third heaven is the abode of God, the angels, and departed saints. A few suggest that, in God's heaven, there may be differing levels of glory – the third heaven being the greatest of these.

14 2 Corinthians 12:2-4

15 See Genesis 5:24 and 2 Kings 2:11

"Then as I looked, I saw a door standing open in heaven," writes the apostle John, "and the same voice I had heard before spoke to me like a trumpet blast. The voice said, 'Come up here, and I will show you what must happen after this.' And instantly I was in the Spirit, and I saw a throne in heaven and someone sitting on it."[16] John's experience was different to Paul's. He knew exactly what happened – he was caught up to heaven in spirit, his body remaining on earth.

Both men received incredible revelation of things in heaven and things to come. One kept silent and one wrote down what he saw.

Today, some discredit those having visions of heaven and speaking about it, citing Paul's silence. They ignore the fact that John revealed almost all that he saw (as did Ezekiel, Isaiah, and Micaiah), forever recorded in the book of Revelation. The lesson is that there will be times when it would be wise to remain silent and times to speak about what one has seen. The Holy Spirit will give us wisdom if we ask him.

Whether by vision or visitation, all these people saw wondrous things, some of which they were permitted to tell others about. This is happening to many believers, including children, all over the earth today. There is a door opening into the heavens. These experiences can occur in the body, out of body, or in a vision. Visions seem to be the most common way. These visions can, at times, be so vivid that the person feels as if they are there. It works like this: think about a great memory of a wonderful holiday, a special moment with family or friends, or an exciting event. Close your eyes and picture it

---

16 Revelation 4:1-2

again. You see, hear, feel, and smell. You are accessing a place by memory. Your body and spirit is in the present, but you are there in the past. In the same way, the Holy Spirit can enable us to access a place by revelation and it feels like you are there seeing, hearing, and feeling it.

"The Spirit lifted me up between earth and heaven," writes Ezekiel the prophet, "and in visions of God he took me to Jerusalem."[17] Ezekiel here describes a vision in which God transported him from Babylon, where he was an exile, to the city of Jerusalem in Israel. While his body remained in Babylon, he went to another place on earth in a vision. In the New Testament, Phillip the evangelist met an Ethiopian royal official on the road from Jerusalem to Gaza, led him to the Lord, and then the Spirit snatched him away bodily to the town of Azotus, some thirty kilometres away.[18] If the Holy Spirit can do this in the earthly realm, he can also do it in the heavenly realm, and transport a person, by vision or visitation, into heaven, and reveal its glory to him or her.

Heaven's Mansions

Sometime after my first vision, I had another vision in which I saw Jesus in heaven. He stood on a path, his face and clothing again radiating light so brilliant, that I could scarcely look at him. He said, "Come," and we walked together along the path until we came to a high stone wall with an arched wooden door. I knew that it was somewhere in the city of God. An angel opened the door and we entered the most beautiful

---

17 Ezekiel 8:3 (NIV)

18 See Acts 8:39-40

garden I have ever seen. The lawn was perfect and vivid green, surrounded by beautiful trees laden with gorgeous looking fruit, some of which were unlike anything seen on earth. One tree had oval-shaped purple fruit with long, twisted filaments springing artistically from them. A fountain stood at the centre of the garden, while flowers of exquisite beauty and dazzling colours filled the borders.

Jesus told me that this was his garden of delights, a place of intimacy with him. I then realised we were in the back garden of a magnificent mansion, which I took to be Jane's. We entered through the back door and I could see that there were many rooms, but no kitchen. (I thought to myself that either God provides all the food in heaven, people there don't need food until they get their resurrection bodies, or the kitchens are in the men's mansions as a kind of justice to women!) The rooms appeared to be places where people met. I saw a library and Jesus explained that it contained books of earth history – past, present, and future. He told me that Jane often read them and that was how she accumulated knowledge.

Then I noticed a sweeping staircase leading up to the next floor. Jane stood at the top and was clothed in a beautiful, pure white robe. She looked young and perfect. She came down the stairs and seemed so pleased to see me. I felt such incredible love from her. I knew that after I complete my work on earth, I would join her in heaven. The three of us then strolled out to the garden of delights where the Lord said he met with Jane often. After I said goodbye to her, Jesus and I walked out of the garden and onto the path. As we walked along, I asked how I could cope with the loneliness until I joined Jane in heaven or perhaps remarried. Jesus turned to me and said, "Wait, be strong, and let your heart take courage, wait!"

Then he told me that it was time to return and the vision ended.

The date was January 15th, the first wedding anniversary after Jane's death. Many had warned me that in the first year after the death of a loved one, birthdays, anniversaries, and other special occasions could be especially hard to handle. The Lord's kindness in granting me this vision helped me to navigate that day with great joy.

Afterwards I thought, *Did I make all this up? Was it real?* Yet there were details beyond my mind's natural ability to manufacture. Sometime later, I read an account of a Korean woman's visions of heaven, in which she describes being shown around a castle: "The sliding glass door did not lead into another room; rather it was the doorway to the castle's garden. In the centre of this glorious place, there was a pond. The entire 'back yard' was surrounded by a rock wall. Flowers of every type and description formed a sea of beauty everywhere I looked. I noticed that a variety of fruit trees grew close to the wall. These trees were filled with the biggest, most luscious-looking fruit I'd ever seen."[19]

Soon after, someone related an American prophet's vision of heaven: "I saw an open door that never closed, which went into a library full of books. I saw numerous people in the library. They took down books off the shelves: books of the past, books of the present, and books of the future." Marvelling at the similarity of these visions to mine, I concluded that what I had seen was a true glimpse of heaven.

---

19 Choo Thomas, *Heaven is So Real*, Lake Mary, Charisma House, 2006, p.27

But Isn't this Talking to the Dead?

Critics of these experiences often reject them as attempts by grieving individuals to talk to dead loved ones (necromancy). And indeed the Bible does forbid such things. "Someone may say to you, "Let's ask the mediums and those who consult the spirits of the dead. With their whisperings and mutterings, they will tell us what to do.'" records the prophet Isaiah. "But shouldn't people ask God for guidance? Should the living seek guidance from the dead?"[20] God gave Moses similar instructions, "Do not let your people practice fortune-telling, or use sorcery, or interpret omens, or engage in witchcraft, or cast spells, or function as mediums or psychics, or call forth the spirits of the dead."[21]

Clearly, the Lord forbids such practices and calls them an abomination, and for good reason.

To seek the dead for comfort or guidance through spiritualism, séances or mediums, is deceptive and not to be trusted. Familiar spirits – demons that are acquainted or familiar with the dead person – masquerade as the deceased soul, cleverly mimicking them, thus fooling the living into thinking that they really are talking to their departed loved ones. This is deadly and not only opens the person to demonisation but may also allow the evil spirit to inject a false prophetic picture of the person's future. There may be truth in what the spirit says, but there will be just enough error to make it poisonous and harmful. The most common deception is the false hope that a person can make it to heaven without Christ.

---

20 Isaiah 8:19
21 Deuteronomy 18:10-11

Some may cite the Old Testament incident where a desperate King Saul used a medium to contact the dead prophet Samuel to obtain guidance, as legitimising the use of mediums.[22] God overruled, however, and permitted the real Samuel to appear to Saul, rather than a familiar spirit. The medium shrieked in terror at this. And the message that Samuel gave Saul was not at all encouraging, but a withering judgment: "Tomorrow you will be in the place of the dead with me."

God does not permit the spirits of the dead to contact the living. Jesus taught this. In the story of the rich man and the beggar,[23] both die at a similar time. Lazarus, the beggar, is comforted in Paradise with Abraham while the fires of hell torment the rich man. Addressing Abraham, the rich man says, "I beg you, father, send Lazarus to my family, for I have five brothers. Let him warn them, so that they will not also come to this place of torment." Abraham replied, "They have Moses and the Prophets; let them listen to them."

No, father Abraham," he said, "but if someone from the dead goes to them, they will repent."

"If they do not listen to Moses and the Prophets," answered Abraham, "they will not be convinced even if someone rises from the dead."

God expects us to get our revelation and comfort from the Bible and his Holy Spirit, not the dead. However, in special circumstances that are under the control of the Holy Spirit, it is possible to have encounters, and communication with dead

22 See 1 Samuel 28
23 See Luke 16:19-31 (NIV)

believers (who are not really dead but simply living in another dimension). One such instance occurred in the ministry of Jesus. "About eight days later Jesus took Peter, John, and James up on a mountain to pray," records the Gospel of Luke, "and as he was praying, the appearance of his face was transformed, and his clothes became dazzling white. Suddenly, two men, Moses and Elijah, appeared and began talking with Jesus. They were glorious to see. And they were speaking about his exodus from this world, which was about to be fulfilled in Jerusalem."[24] Moses had died around fourteen hundred years earlier, while God had translated Elijah to heaven some eight hundred years before.

In the Apostle John's visitation into heaven, he sees a scroll that no one is worthy to open. "Then I began to weep bitterly," he writes, "because no one was found worthy to open the scroll and read it. But one of the twenty-four elders said to me, 'Stop weeping! Look, the Lion of the tribe of Judah, the heir to David's throne, has won the victory. He is worthy to open the scroll and its seven seals.'"[25] According to Revelation chapter four, the twenty-four elders are clothed in white, wear golden crowns, and sit on thrones surrounding the throne of God. As only believers are destined to reign with God, these elders cannot be angels, but must be believers. Whether John was seeing them as in his day, or was looking into the future is uncertain. The point is, while in a visitation into heaven, he heard a dead believer speak to him.

Later John hears the voices of many martyrs (those who had died for their faith in Christ, but who were now alive in

---

24 Luke 9:28-31
25 Revelation 5:4-5

heaven) crying out for justice before God's throne. "I saw under the altar the souls of all who had been martyred for the word of God and for being faithful in their testimony," he records. "They shouted to the Lord and said, 'O Sovereign Lord, holy and true, how long before you judge the people who belong to this world and avenge our blood for what they have done to us?'"[26] There are other instances in John's revelation in which he hears the believers in heaven speaking.

It seems that when the Holy Spirit grants a vision of, or visitation into, heaven, people may encounter deceased believers who communicate with them. If God is orchestrating it, it is legitimate. The church, however, has struggled with this over the centuries as Francis McNutt attests: "The saints, of course, were considered to be living in heaven ... there are numerous records [in early church history] about how the saints often appeared in visions, but they belonged to another world, and attempts to contact them directly were forbidden as spiritualism."[27] This forbidding of contacting the dead stemmed from the post-Constantine church where increasing Greek influence led Christians to despise the present physical life and so glorify the heavens that they considered the thought of heaven speaking to this loathsome realm as abhorrent.

Later, however, the reverse happened. A cult of saint worship sprang up, where deceased saints, often seen in visions, were not only worshipped but prayed to, something expressly forbidden by scripture, as Jesus is our only mediator with God. "For there is one God and one mediator between God and mankind," warns the Bible, "the man Christ Jesus."[28]

---

26 Revelation 6:9-10

27 Francis McNutt, *The Healing Reawakening*, Grand Rapids, Chosen Books, 2005, p.112

28 1 Timothy 2:5 (NIV)

God thus prohibits the desire to contact dead believers, or give them an importance beyond that which he intended. However, if in our seeking of the Lord, he permits us to see the realities of heaven, including, at times, encounters with heavenly believers, this is allowable. For me, the visions I have described, and others the Lord gave me, together with my study of scripture, supernaturally accelerated my recovery from grief. I began to sing, "You have turned my mourning into joyful dancing. You have taken away my clothes of mourning and clothed me with joy, that I might sing praises to you and not be silent. O LORD my God, I will give you thanks forever!"[29]

"The person who successfully grieves," explains a grief counsellor, "does not forget the lost loved one. Nor are they free from hurt or pain at all times. When their grief is through, the person has let go of what they once had and has made a new pattern of living. This will include new places for putting energy and focusing effort, new attachments for emotional satisfaction, perhaps new relationships. In this, the past is not forgotten."[30] The memory of the loved one does not fade, but the pain of their loss does.

Some five months after Jane's death, my heart was feeling whole and healed, to the point that I removed my wedding ring, and even entertained the thought of remarriage. Little did I know that circumstances were unfolding that would allow God to make this happen.

---

29 Psalm 30:11-12

30 *Understanding Grief and Loss* workbook, Blueprint Centre for Learning, 2007, p.31. Used by permission.

chapter four

GRETA'S STORY

"Greta, come quickly! Ron has collapsed!"

The urgency in Chris' voice instantly geared me into high alert. Perplexed by this unexpected phone call, I leapt into action nonetheless. Shoving the partly prepared evening meal into the fridge, I called to my son David who was in his bedroom: "Something's happened to Dad. He's at the bowling club." In the summer months after work, Ron and his friend Chris would regularly swim off Browns Bay beach on Auckland's North Shore and have refreshments at the club afterwards.

I asked David to drive so that I could phone his older brother, Joshua, who was at a part-time student job. Fortunately, the drive down into the Bay was a brief five minutes. As we pulled into the car park, I saw Chris waiting outside the door of the club for me. I jumped out and ran inside after him while David parked the car. The scene that greeted me was shocking. Ron lay deeply unconscious on the floor and a paramedic was on his knees beside him performing CPR. I had only one thought:

save his life! I knew I had to stay calm. There was no time for emotionalism. Joining the paramedic on the floor I said, "I'm a physiotherapist. Can I help?"

"Yes, please," he replied. "Operate the ambubag while I keep doing the chest compressions. The rest of the team will be here soon in an ambulance." I was grateful for my emergency hospital training. As we coordinated our actions together, I also was continually praying in tongues under my breath, fighting in prayer for my husband's life. Soon the other paramedics rushed in and took over. They instructed me to move to Ron's feet so that I could hold his legs in elevation, thereby assisting blood flow. The gravity of Ron's condition became apparent – after twenty minutes, he still did not have a stable pulse in spite of applying electric shocks to his chest a few times. As soon as the paramedics achieved a semblance of stability, they whisked him into the waiting ambulance and sped to North Shore Hospital Emergency Department. As they were leaving, I eyeballed the senior paramedic and said, "Don't give up." He looked straight back at me and replied, "We won't." I knew he meant it.

As David and I travelled to the hospital, I phoned a number of friends to set up a prayer chain. Outside the hospital, we met Joshua, who had hurried from work, and went in together. The senior paramedic was just leaving the emergency room where Ron lay on a bed. "We did everything we could and never gave up," he said with compassion. I thanked him for giving Ron the best chance possible. Told to stand at the back of the room, we watched silently as each member of the emergency team worked quickly and purposefully. While one briskly cut Ron's trouser legs and shirt as the fastest way to remove them, others intubated him, inserted drips and applied monitor pads to his chest. Surrounded by this intense activity, Ron was oblivious, in a deep coma. Once all their tasks were complete, they told me that Ron would be transferred to the specialist cardiac unit at Auckland Hospital. Once again, we were driving to yet another hospital.

On arrival, Ron was taken immediately into theatre where the surgeons inserted a stent into the blocked artery that had caused the massive cardiac arrest and his sudden collapse. The boys and I were ushered into a room to wait. It was to be a long night. The fateful phone call had come at about 6pm that balmy Friday summer evening. It was near midnight when Ron emerged from theatre and they wheeled him into the intensive care unit (ICU). The doctor explained that they had put Ron into an induced coma to optimise the medical outcome. The empathetic nursing staff said that I was welcome to stay the night in the waiting room. I urged the boys, together with a few of their supportive friends who had joined us, to go home and get a good night's sleep. Alone, and straddled over several seats, I slept fitfully, intermittently interceding to Father. The night passed uneventfully.

Early the next morning, Joshua and David returned with their close friends. After medical rounds, the specialist took the three of us into a consulting room. He explained that Ron's heart was so badly damaged, that it was unlikely to sustain life. A further critical problem was possible brain damage due to sustained oxygen deprivation. The neurological assessment was not at all good. In short, the news was bleak. The medical team would make a final assessment and decision on Sunday, after slowly taking Ron out of the induced coma through the morning. As Ron was presently stable, and so heavily drugged that he was unable to hear us, the specialist advised us to go home to rest. He assured me that they would contact me immediately if any change in Ron's condition occurred.

After we arrived home, more of the boys' friends arrived and arranged an impromptu barbecue for us. Having known them for years, we regarded these friends as part of our family. I was moved by their love and loyalty – they simply hung out and were there for us. As we sat around the pool, I shared what I believed in my heart – that with God nothing was impossible. He had the power to miraculously raise Ron up to complete health, despite the poor medical prognosis, and this was what I was asking Father for. I had faith to believe God's Word, especially as I had seen the dead raised to life in Africa where we used to live.

The Day That Changed My Life

Sunday dawned bright and sunny, belying the tumultuous drama unfolding in our lives. As we returned to the hospital through largely deserted streets, I was acutely aware this was D-day. Some hours later, when Ron had been brought out of unconsciousness, and the final neurological assessment completed, we were again called into a consulting room. The specialist was kind and frank in his verbal report. Unexpectedly and surprisingly, Ron's heart was miraculously beating strongly with a perfect wave pattern. However, neurological damage was too severe to sustain life. He had zero reflexes below the neck, could not see, and once disconnected from the ventilator that was artificially breathing for him, unlikely to breathe on his own. The doctor suggested we spend a few hours with Ron saying our farewells.

It was at that moment that I knew the Lord was going to heal Ron, not the way we desperately wanted, but by taking him home to heaven. I contained all the emotions flooding my mind. I needed to stay strong for my precious husband – I needed to minister to him. As we were ushered into the ICU, I was thankful to God for the opportunity for my sons and me to spend this time with Ron. The miracle healing of his heart enabled this. We all took turns chatting to him, expressing our love and how much he meant to us. I read Bible verses, prayed aloud over him, sang worship songs, and the presence of the Lord filled the room. A number of friends came to say goodbye and left. Four close friends remained. They prayed and sang with us. Even though Ron could not physically respond, I knew he could hear every word. This was especially obvious when I asked our friends to sing *Amazing Grace* with me, as it was his favourite hymn. Ron began moving his eyelids and his head side to side, the only part of his body not paralysed. Our friends also commented on the tangible presence of God bathing Ron and filling the room.

Then it was time. I kissed Ron's forehead and said, "I love you so much, sweetheart. I let you go. Go home to Jesus." My eyes blurred with tears. About twenty seconds after the staff switched the ventilator off, Ron was gone, but the peace of the Lord's presence remained. "Mom, did you see?" observed Joshua. "As you spoke those words, Dad's eyes suddenly focused and he looked at you and saw you for a few seconds before he drifted into unconsciousness and passed away." How kind of Father to grant Ron a final glimpse of the wife he deeply loved. Joshua, David and I wept together. From this day on, our lives would be forever changed.

Where It All Began

Born in the Northern Cape Province of South Africa, in the sunny city of Kimberley, I was blessed with a happy childhood, being raised and nurtured by God-fearing parents in a loving, secure home. The city was small enough to foster a strong sense of community, and I recall spending much time in spontaneous group outdoor activities as well as organised sport, balanced with indoor delights of books, creative pastimes and my mom's delicious home-baking! It was a safe environment in which to grow up. Just as well, as my adventurous spirit loved to freely wander off on exploratory 'expeditions' beyond the city boundaries.

It is interesting to note how many cities across the globe acquire nicknames. Kimberley was no exception. Worldwide she is known famously as the *City of Diamonds*. She is also renowned for *The Big Hole*, claimed to be the largest hand-dug hole on the planet. The discovery of diamonds in the 1870s birthed the city, as fortune seekers flocked from overseas nations. To extract these abundant precious gems, they dug until there was an enormous open pit the size of eight football fields.

Down through the generations, diamonds shaped and influenced many spheres of life there. The school anthem of both boys' and girls' high schools was themed around diamonds. It starts with this line: "The diamonds of our city are sent across the seas … " Then the anthem declares that her sons and daughters likewise are sent across the seas to other nations. Decades later, I was to discover how prophetic this was for my life. De Beers Consolidated Mines, the world's largest diamond mining company, was founded and had their headquarters, in Kimberley. They offered extremely generous all-expenses-paid university scholarships, one to each of three local high schools. On a personal level, I was the grateful recipient at Kimberley Girls' High School.

On finishing school at the age of eighteen, I left home and travelled the almost one thousand kilometres south, to the historic University of Cape Town, South Africa's oldest university, set on the lower slopes of majestic Table Mountain. This famed flat-topped mountain, home to about twenty-two hundred unique plant species, forms the backdrop to the *Mother City*, as Cape Town is fondly nicknamed. My new abode in a women's residence gave me splendid views of the mountain and, filled with excitement, I commenced my four-year degree.

The Decision

One evening in the September of my first year, I made what would prove to be the most important decision of my life. A few weeks earlier, two fellow students had dragged me reluctantly to a campus crusade where Michael Green, a British evangelist, had been invited to speak. Unbeknown to me, his topic *Freedom* deposited a seed into my spirit. Many questions pertaining to the meaning of life began to fill my thoughts. Then, while studying for upcoming exams this particular evening, suddenly the presence of God filled my room. I heard Jesus quietly say to me, "Greta, you have come to a crossroads in your life. You must choose to either go your own way or follow me."

Encountering his presence was so real that my decision was immediate. At that moment, I fully believed Jesus to be the Son of God and the Saviour of the world. I received him into my life. Instinctively I knew that true freedom could only be found in

Jesus. Soon after, I was filled with the Holy Spirit and baptised in water. And so began a relationship far more precious than all the diamonds from *The Big Hole*, and that will continue forever in a City[1] far more beautiful than Cape Town.

Successfully armed with my Bachelor of Science Degree (Physiotherapy), and firmly founded in basic Christian teachings, thanks to the substantial and vibrant Christian student groups, and resources on campus, I ventured into my new world of work. I found a small studio apartment within walking distance of Groote Schuur Hospital, where I would join the ranks of the Physiotherapy Department. Renowned as the institution where the first heart transplant in the world was conducted by Professor Christiaan Barnard, this large teaching hospital, where I had trained as an undergraduate, offered excellent experience in every field of physiotherapy. This included the transplant unit where a few of us were trained in this specialist area.

Every day was a pronounced learning curve, not only in the stimulating environment of my work, but also in all spheres of my life. I enjoyed becoming more involved in Harfield Road Assembly of God Church, which I had attended as a student. It was here at a young adults' barbecue that I met Ron. I was so focused on delighting myself in the Lord[2] that the moment took me by surprise. Soon after we started dating, I heard the Holy Spirit whisper clearly, "This is the man you are going to marry." Ron soon stole my heart and seven months later, we wed!

---

1 See chapter 15
2 See Psalm 37:4

The Adventure Continues

The great adventure of marriage, and sharing life together, had begun. We designed and built our own home, and while I worked, did postgraduate studies and lectured at the university, Ron successfully grew his fledgling business with entrepreneurial flair. The joy of being in love was augmented by the birth of two beautiful baby boys just twenty-two months apart. As I delighted in being a wife, I relished motherhood too. My cup was full to overflowing. The years that followed were blessed with much joy and fulfilment, mixed with hard work, challenges and the common trials that face every family.

In early 1995, several months after celebrating South Africa's first all-inclusive elections, we were dismayed to observe a fast-spreading lawlessness and rising rampant crime. The country of my birth was no longer a safe environment to raise children. Ron and I began to pray, asking the Lord where he wanted us to live geographically on the planet. I knew that if he told us to stay, he would protect our lives. After a consistent period of seeking his will for our family, God said, "Go to New Zealand. I tell you, go." It was absolutely clear; I knew that I knew it was right. The Lord also highlighted the following verse from Jeremiah 29:11 personally to us, "For I know the plans I have for you, declares the LORD, plans to prosper you and not to harm you, plans to give you hope and a future."[3] And he confirmed it a few times. For example, the next Sunday at church, the pastor preached a message using this same scripture. The following week we received an unexpected letter from friends in a distant city. They wrote, "We don't know why, but we feel we should send you this scripture." It was Jeremiah 29:11!

---

3 Jeremiah 29:11 (NIV)

Although there was a huge price tagged to our decision, we were willing to pay it and believed that obeying God was always worth it. Within two years, we emigrated half-way around the world to an unknown country. The Lord gave me great grace to let go all I held dear in South Africa – our home, family and friends, the vast spectacular natural beauty, and the deep roots of my heritage. God enabled me to be grateful for all his goodness in the past, to begin a whole new chapter in our lives, and to look to the future, entrusting it into his hands.

I shall never forget the moment my feet first touched New Zealand soil. To my amazement, I felt familiarly at home. To this day, I am thankful for my internationally-recognised physiotherapy qualification that opened the door for us to receive residency in this beautiful little nation. We began to rebuild our lives afresh. As we started from scratch in almost all aspects, I determined to enjoy the huge learning and adapting process so that, as good citizens, we became an integrated part of society. Before I knew it, this became an established reality. As Ron and I worked very hard, God our Provider blessed the work of our hands.

The years flew by. While I ran my private practice, Ron completed postgraduate computer studies and environmental health qualifications, so that he worked part-time as a consultant in this field, while also gradually developing his import/distribution business. Juggling the necessity to earn a living, we still tried to prioritise family times as best we could. I remember one such day: very early on this mid-January morning, Ron and I slipped out to a nearby beach, leaving our university student sons to sleep in. After twenty-eight years of marriage, we loved the companionship of being together even more.

We walked the length of the beach hand-in-hand chatting, then followed the track at the far end as it wound up to the cliff top. We sat down on a shady bench to enjoy the spectacular view of sun-dazzled sea and prayed together, thanking the Lord for all his goodness to us and for his beautiful creation. This would be the final weekend I would ever share with my husband. I am so thankful for that special day of love and closeness that remains in my memory. The following Friday, Ron suffered his fatal heart attack.

The Road of Grief

Grief is an overwhelming all-pervading thing, and the unexpected suddenness of our world being torn apart left our boys and me reeling with shock.

With one traumatic blow my precious husband and best friend, and our boys' deeply loved father and mentor was gone, leaving a gaping hole in our hearts that felt as huge the Kimberley Big Hole. What do you do with this deluge of pain and sorrow? Where do you go? There was only one place I knew. I ran to Jesus. I ran into his open arms and clung to him for dear life. Mine had fallen apart and I had no idea what my and my sons' futures held. However, I knew my Lord was holding us, and our destinies too. With abandon, I poured out my grief and my tears in his embrace and I chose to worship him and Father. In the weeks and months that followed, I would daily spend any free time alone in his presence. I would weep and worship, I would pray and sing praises to my God. And he ministered his love and peace to my aching soul.

That first Monday morning as a widow, I thanked him for fulfilling a wonderful biblical promise to me: "Take delight in the Lord, and he will give you the desires of your heart."[4] He had truly fulfilled my desires, with the joyous, deep bonds of love in my marriage to this special man and in blessing us with two fine sons.

"Heavenly Father," I said, "I trust in your sovereign wisdom, that you work all things together for the good of those who love you, and that taking Ron to heaven is your divine will. Thank you he is healed, whole, and full of joy in your face-to-face presence. I love you, Lord." Father assured me, "My precious daughter, Ron has run his race and completed his course on earth. This is my perfect timing to bring him home. He is with me and Jesus."

The apostle Paul calls God "the Father of compassion and the God of all comfort, who comforts us in all our trouble."[5] I experienced the reality of this truth like never before in my life. Father's supernatural comfort infused my being and I felt physically cocooned, like cotton wool, in his compassion. He graced me to make the many arrangements for the funeral, held four days later. I was so thankful for the loving support and many deeds of practical help from dear friends, such as bringing us home-cooked meals, phoning all my patients to postpone appointments to a week later, driving me places, and so on.

As the one who knew Ron more deeply than anyone else, and so could best represent him, I asked the Lord for his strength to be the main speaker at his celebration service. The opening song I chose was Matt Redman's *Blessed be Your Name*. It would

---

4 Psalm 37:4 (NIV)
5 2 Corinthians 1:3b-4 (NIV)

become my daily theme song for many weeks ahead. A pastor friend graciously travelled a long distance to deliver an anointed gospel message, which was Ron's wish. The large number of people who attended, and the tributes paid to Ron by my sons and others, greatly moved me. In my weakness, God's strong hand and presence were upon the whole day from start to finish.

After the funeral, being self-employed necessitated my quick return to work. In addition, I had to continue to run Ron's business for the time being. The only way to survive was to live in complete dependency on the Holy Spirit. 'Cling and sing' summarised my journey through the deepest grief I had ever experienced. The psalmist aptly described it, "On my bed I remember you; I think of you through the watches of the night. Because you are my help, I sing in the shadow of your wings. I cling to you; your right hand upholds me."[6] Faced with overwhelming challenges, I frequently cried out to God for help and he faithfully gave me wisdom to prioritise impossibly long to-do lists, and supernatural strength to sustain fifteen-hour working days.

I quickly learned to live one day at a time. During the day, he enabled me to competently care for, and treat, my patients. During the night, alone in the bed Ron and I once shared, I grieved. About four months' later, relief arrived in the form of my younger brother, Neil. He and his family had 'coincidently' planned to relocate from Canada to New Zealand, and I gratefully handed over the reins of Ron's business into his capable hands.

The nights were also 'encounter' times with the Lord. His tangible presence made me secure. Jesus often reminded me

---

[6] Psalm 63: 6-8 (NIV)

that he was with me. He would speak reassuring words, and powerful prophetic promises. He gave me dreams and visions of heaven. Many a time I would wake up, realising I had been singing songs in my sleep to him, like the chorus *Immanuel* which declares that God is with us. During this period, he was gently renewing vision in me. Jeremiah 29:11 had been his word to Ron and me as a couple. Now I sensed him say it was specifically for me in this new season of my life. As I kept delighting in him and following him with my whole heart, he would fulfil my desires with good things in his time, desires not consciously formulated, but buried somewhere under my grief and pain. When I look back, I see a continuous thread of thankfulness and rejoicing, in spite of the frequent tears and deep loss I felt. It was solely God's amazing gift of grace that empowered me to do this. I would only fully realise, much later, that this was a vital key to sustain me on my grief journey, and to come through at the other end.

And come through I did. It happened in a miraculous moment. About five months after Ron had passed away, I was alone, waiting on the Lord. Suddenly I felt him touch me, and I knew my broken heart was supernaturally healed and made whole. The pain and grief was gone. The gratitude for happy memories remained and a new joy filled me. The next day the Lord downloaded two detailed pages of his future plans for my life. Father finished with these words, "See, I have told you ahead of time that you may know the plans and purposes I have for you. I love you, my child, with an everlasting love." It left me in awe and wonder at our great Almighty God who stoops down to so tenderly take care of each one of us.

Events were about to unfold quickly, just as he said they would.

chapter five

GOD THE MATCHMAKER

It was a wonderful trip. My son Tim and I had enjoyed six weeks visiting various destinations in America, Europe and Asia. Desiring to see me refreshed after all the years of caring for Jane, the church I attended had kindly taken an offering to send me on a world tour. They raised enough to send two people, and not wanting to travel alone, I had asked my youngest son to accompany me. Two months had passed since I had taken off my wedding ring, and seven months since Jane had passed away.

As the Boeing 777 neared New Zealand, my thoughts drifted back to all the exciting things we had done on the trip: taking a cruise on San Francisco's beautiful harbour, touring London with its ornate old buildings, exploring the quaint villages and leafy countryside of Devon and Cornwall, journeying by train under the English Channel to Paris, climbing the Eiffel Tower, and strolling along the Champs Elysees with its cafes and shops spilling out onto the street, drinking in the lush sights of Provence, and finally being caught up in the mad rush of Hong Kong. We had also included a number of places that Jane, originally from England, had often told me about: Plymouth, where she trained to be a cardiac technician, her family's home in nearby Ivybridge, the tiny Cornish fishing villages which she had often visited on holiday, and the atmospheric Journey's End in Ringmore, Devon – an inn built in 1300AD where the doorway is so short that, to get in, you have to 'duck or grouse' as the locals say. Seeing these places, and walking in Jane's footsteps, had brought an even greater sense of closure to me.

Soon, the thud of the aircraft's undercarriage being lowered into the slipstream jolted me back to the present. As the plane was about to land at Auckland International Airport, I quietly declared, "Lord, I am in a new season. No longer is it a season of hope deferred, but one of desires fulfilled. And part of this season is meeting someone new. Please bring her to me, as I am not going looking. You brought Eve to Adam, and I believe that you will do the same for me."

Three separate events, some weeks before I left for overseas, had given me the confidence to pray this way. One day, as I read the story of the patriarch Jacob meeting his future wife Rachel, I noted with interest the Bible's description of her: "Rachel was beautiful in every way, with a lovely face and shapely figure."[1] Though I had probably read it many times, I had never paid much attention to this verse before. It was as if it had been hiding in the Bible all the time, waiting for me to discover it. I thought to myself that I would like my next wife to be exactly like that. So I prayed, "I'd like to order a Rachel please, Lord!"

Later, a prophetic friend said to me, "I sense that your next wife will not be New Zealand born, but will be from overseas."

---

1 Genesis 29:17 (NLT 1996 version)

A little while after this, as I was falling asleep one night, I saw a vision of a woman in my mind. Tall and slim, her long black hair was pulled back and framed a youthful face with high cheekbones, and a pleasant smile. She wore a white blouse and cardigan, over a floral print pencil skirt, and calf-length dark brown leather boots. She looked lovely. As I fell asleep, I wondered what this could mean. During the night, the same vision came twice more, and I concluded that she may possibly be my future wife. Thankfully, I never met such a person on the trip, as I had wanted to concentrate on sightseeing, not romance.

Five days after arriving home, I went to church to do a lecture for the Bible College. The dean of students greeted me with a rather sheepish look and a letter in his hand.

"I'm sorry," he said, as he handed over the envelope.

"Why, what have you done?"

"This came three months ago and remained hidden in one of my files until I rediscovered it. Here it is."

Curious, I completed the lecture and then read the letter. It was very moving – from a woman called Greta whom I had never met. I will let Greta explain why she wrote to me, but need to clarify something first. One of the first messages I had preached after Jane's death was entitled *Blessed be Your Name,* reflecting the impact that Matt Redman's song of the same name had had on me. In my sermon, I spoke about what I had learned in my time of great loss, how God had turned that loss to gain, and the glorious hope of heaven. My eldest son Joseph suggested that we put the video recording of the message on my website. I was reluctant to do so, fearing that it was too personal. Joseph insisted. You know you are getting old, when you have to obey your children! I wanted to change the title to *Turning Your Losses to Gain* but in the end, we agreed that it would be best to leave the title as is. This was to prove an extremely providential move.

Greta

Five weeks after Ron unexpectedly went to heaven, I was still singing Matt Redman's song, *Blessed Be Your Name* every day. One morning while treating a patient, she began speaking about a church she used to attend when she lived in another part of Auckland city. She spoke so highly of this church stream which was unfamiliar to me, that it piqued my interest. That evening I decided to find out more and switched on my computer. In my internet tinkering, I came to a particular website where my attention was suddenly arrested by familiar words: a video sermon entitled, *Blessed Be Your Name!*

The words of this song so echoed my heart that I felt compelled to watch. The unknown pastor shared that he had recently lost his wife of many years. I fully identified. As I listened I heard the very same things the Lord had been speaking to me in my grieving over these past several weeks. How encouraging it was to receive confirmation that I really was hearing God's voice. In addition, this man reiterated the numerous scriptures on heaven I had been meditating on. The Holy Spirit had given me fresh revelation and I was seeing heaven in a whole new light. Heaven was so real to me now, as real as Australia was across the Tasman Sea from New Zealand; unseen to the human eye but there. And the preacher vividly affirmed this.

Strongly impacted by the sermon from this man called David Peters, I felt I must write him a thank-you letter explaining how and why his message meant so much to me. I ended my epistle with this: "God bless you, David. I shall pray for you as I pray for myself, that we may delight ourselves in the Lord, that he will fill the huge holes in our lives with himself and that we will continue to bless his name even as we shed buckets of tears." I sent the letter off with the presumption that David was a busy pastor and thus without expectation of a reply.

David

My message had confirmed so many things that the Lord had also taught Greta, and she was moved to write a thank-you note, which I received three months later. Those three months were critical: if I had received the letter when she sent it, neither of us would have been ready for what was about to happen next. Feeling embarrassed that she had not had the courtesy of a reply, I hurriedly emailed Greta to thank her for the touching letter:

> Dear Greta
> A very embarrassed church staff member handed me your letter yesterday, apologising that he had forgotten to give it to me when it arrived a few months ago. I have been away overseas for a while as well.
> Thank you for writing such a heartfelt letter. I admire your faith in the Lord and the lovely spirit of trust exhibited in the midst of great pain and loss. I am glad my message encouraged you. How are you doing four months' on?
> I find the pain eases but the memories remain, which is a nice thing.
> Blessings, David

Greta replied and, as we started to exchange emails over the next few weeks, something strange began to happen. I could not wait to power up the computer each morning to see if there was a new email from this woman I had never seen or met, but who seemed to have such a soft and beautiful heart. It was like a rerun of the Tom Hanks and Meg Ryan movie, *You've Got Mail*. Could it be that I was falling in love? Not wanting to trust my emotions alone, I remained uncertain, and prayed that the Lord would guide me. What happened next began to remove any doubts that I had.

Two weeks after receiving Greta's letter, while in worship one day, I had a vision of the throne room of heaven. Multitudes of saints worshipped and danced before the Father and the Son, who sat at his right hand. I joined them in worship and then was beckoned to approach the throne. Father smiled at me so welcomingly. Jesus stood, came towards me and embraced me. I could not believe how approachable and welcoming the Lord of glory was, and yet the scripture plainly says, "Because of Christ and our faith in him, we can now come boldly and confidently into God's presence."[2] Jesus and I then walked amongst the saints, discussing how I was doing as we went.

"You are doing well," Jesus encouraged me.

"Thank you Lord," I replied, "but I feel very lonely."

Stopping, Jesus turned towards me and smiled knowingly. At that moment, a young man approached us. He was handsome and muscular, with reddish-brown hair. Addressing me he said, "Take good care of her." Could this be the deceased husband of

---

2 Ephesians 3:12

my future wife? As I pondered this, the vision ended. Recording carefully the details of what I had seen, I kept it all in the back of my mind.

Greta and I continued to exchange emails, and although my love for her was deepening, I found it increasingly strange to relate to someone I had never seen. She had seen photos of Jane and me on my website, but I had no concept of her and Ron. Finally, I plucked up the courage to ask if she could send a photograph of themselves. The photo soon arrived and as I nervously opened the computer file that contained it, my jaw dropped at what I saw. Not only was she beautiful, but she was the woman I had seen in the vision! In the photo, Ron stood next to her with a thick crop of reddish-brown hair! I realised then that this liaison had the hand of God all over it. We continued to correspond and, during that time, the Lord spoke to both of us in additional ways that he was bringing us together.

Greta

After the initial surprise of receiving David's belated reply, I began to enjoy sharing our mutual experiences and challenges. It felt good to bounce about thoughts with a fellow traveller on this road never travelled before. Two things especially impressed me about David: he loved God wholeheartedly and he had faithfully loved his courageous and amazing wife. The more I came to know the person, the more I grew to like and trust him. This man was a kindred spirit. I eagerly looked forward to his next email.

However, when David requested a photograph of Ron and me, I confess to feeling a bit apprehensive. I liked being Miss Anonymity! Four days after sending the photograph, which happened to be Friday 13th, God totally blew such notions out of the water. Whoever coined it an unlucky day got it wrong. It was a profound day of a quantum leap in my life, as described in the previous chapter. During a short lunch break in the midst of a busy day, I stopped to be still with Father. In a moment, his love powerfully healed my broken heart and he filled me with such indescribable joy I felt I could have burst. I floated on cloud nine for many days afterwards.

The next day the Lord proceeded to reveal the specifics of his new future plans for me, that he was in the process of orchestrating. He spoke plainly and without ambiguity. For example, he said, "I have brought you and David together. I have chosen you to be his wife. You and David will be married for I have ordained it. My anointing will rest on you in a new way, that you may be a helpmate in every way for David." He went on to explain that this was directly connected to his Kingdom purposes for our lives. Father also reassured me, "Do not be afraid. I shall speak to David and tell him exactly what I have told you."

Even so, I felt both excited and terrified at the same time. Knowing me inside out, over the ensuing days, God graciously gave me confirmations himself, and also indirectly through godly friends who had no idea of the drama being played out. I confided in an older wise friend, "God has revealed his future plans in this new season in my life. Please will you pray for me that I have heard correctly?"

"Of course I will," she kindly replied.

She came to see me soon afterwards. "While I was reading the Bible, the name David kept leaping out of the passage," she said, "and the name Peters has come to mind. Do you know someone called *David Peters?*"

I nodded dumbfounded. She neither knew David nor had ever heard of him. "This is the man you will marry," she concluded.

Her words thrilled my heart. I admitted that David and I had been corresponding via email for some weeks, and trusted her to keep our growing romance confidential.

Six days later Father spoke this, "My beloved daughter, I have told David plainly that I have chosen you to be his wife. He knows and he will tell you. Be patient and wait for him. It will be as I have said." Father knew that I was an old-fashioned girl and that wild horses would not drag any such confession from my lips. It had to be David who would speak first and make approaches to me, or else I would flee like a gazelle.

David

A few weeks later, we met for the first time. Over a three-hour lunch, we conversed about our backgrounds, our families, and our losses. There were many similarities: each of us had completed science degrees and teaching diplomas (her tertiary and me secondary), had given our lives to Christ around the same time, albeit on opposite sides of the world, had seen our mothers pass away in the same year, and later our fathers also. The similarities did not end there – we both independently ordered the same meal from the menu, and still often do today. It was like meeting my twin. We agreed to have dinner the following week, and, as I drove home, I meditated on God's remarkable orchestrating of events. My thoughts were interrupted only by my middle son Adam calling to see where I was, what Greta was like, and why I had been so long. Talk about role reversal!

During lunch, I had been careful not to mention any of the supernatural revelation the Lord had given me, for fear that it might put undue pressure on Greta. I wanted our relationship to develop naturally. My apprehension about sharing God's revelation to me lasted only until our second date, during which I let slip that I had had a vision of heaven and how wonderful a place it was. Greta asked for more details, and before we knew it, much of God's leading tumbled out from both of us. It was as if heaven was saying, "Come on you two, get on with it!" Not long after this, we were planning our wedding.

When I share our story in public, I like to point out to young people in the audience, "Do not try this at home!" As both Greta and I were married previously for many years, I believe that God could trust us with an extraordinarily fast courtship. My advice to young people is to enjoy getting to know others in groups; take time to develop friendships, and do not rush things. Pray much and seek the counsel of others. Choosing a life partner is one of the most important decisions a person can make, and should be made carefully and prayerfully. I think in Greta's and my case, God was moving quickly, to position us for the ministry he was about to launch us into.

Greta

I did need to be patient, and wait until our second date, when David shared everything God had revealed to him about us. It was a relief to come clean and confess my own prophetic revelation that dovetailed with his. Comparing timelines in our journals, Father had spoken to David on the exact date he told me he had! There were no doubts. We both knew God the Master Matchmaker was at work in our hearts, stirring a deepening love for each other.

David

Our next step was to win the support of our children. With my sons, any thoughts they had that we may have been rushing things soon evaporated when they met Greta for the first time, as they could see what a lovely person she was and how happy she made me. Greta introduced me to her boys, Joshua and David, and I took an instant liking to them. Sometime later, I took them aside and explained that I loved their mother very much, could not replace their dad, and would like their blessing to marry their mum. They replied, "We couldn't think of anyone better to marry her."

Another thing that helped was our decision to talk freely about Ron and Jane to each other and to our children. We felt secure enough in God's love that it was not uncomfortable for me to hear Greta talk about Ron, or for her to hear me speak about Jane. Because of insecurity, some couples make the mistake of never mentioning their former spouses, and this can deeply hurt their children. A wise counsellor confirmed our decision when he told us, "The degree to which you speak about Ron and Jane, will be the degree to which your sons accept your new relationship."

Some six months after receiving Greta's letter, we were married. On a perfect spring day, friends and family watched as Greta walked down the aisle, escorted by her brother Neil. Dressed in a full length, electric blue gown, with her long black hair falling in waves to below her shoulders, she looked stunningly beautiful. I smiled to myself as I remembered asking the Lord for a Rachel. He had certainly delivered!

Prior to us exchanging vows, the marriage celebrant turned to our five sons, and asked if they would give their blessing to our marriage. All five stood and replied, "Yes we do." One year and ten days after farewelling my first bride, I welcomed my second bride into my life. For Greta it was even shorter – a mere ten months after saying goodbye to her first husband, she joined with her second.

God can heal grief supernaturally, and bring restoration of what is lost. In our case, he did exactly that, and for a second time in our lives, we knew the thrilling joy of true love. He really is the God who makes bitter waters sweet.

chapter six

HE MAKES THE BITTER WATERS SWEET

The dust cloud rose high in the sky as two million or so Israelites marched their way into the arid desert. Having just experienced one of the most extraordinary miracles of history – the crossing of the Red Sea and the destruction of the pursuing Egyptian army – they had set out triumphantly into the wilderness ahead of them.

However, the fierce heat beat down upon them mercilessly, and as each day dragged on, they grew weary. Worse, their water supply had dwindled to threateningly low levels. Scouts were sent ahead to look for any source of the priceless liquid.

Finally, a report arrived that they had found a pool of water. Anticipation rippled through the camp, the people's steps quickening as they followed the scouts to the place they would later name Marah.

As the first of them scooped the water into their mouths, horror seized them. It was poisoned and undrinkable.

"They travelled in this desert for three days without finding any water," records the Bible. "When they came to the oasis of Marah, the water was too bitter to drink. So they called the place Marah (which means bitter)."[1] What cruel disappointment as they tasted the poisoned waters. They had journeyed from a place of triumph, through the desert, to an oasis where they anticipated cool, refreshing waters.

Life can be like this. We may set out on life's journey with high expectations, only to eventually experience disappointments and troubles: sorrow instead of joy, sickness instead of health, frustration instead of a meaningful vocation, failure instead of a successful career, the pain of divorce instead of a blessed marriage, or children who reject God, instead of walking with him. These are all bitter waters. And the most bitter of all is the death of a loved one, or any serious loss for that matter, and the grief that follows. It is in this place, more than any other, that we need to know that God can make bitter waters sweet.

How Does This Happen?

"Then the people complained and turned against Moses. 'What are we going to drink?' they demanded. So Moses cried out to the Lord for help, and the Lord showed him a piece of wood. Moses threw it into the water and this made the water good to drink."[2] The people grumbled. Moses cried out to the Lord.

1 Exodus 15:22-23
2 Exodus 15:24-25

These are the two typical responses to bitter waters: either we let them embitter us and thus complain, or we cry out to God for his perspective and solution. Moses did the right thing. One of his prayers is recorded in Psalm 90.

Did he pray this at Marah? We cannot say for certain, but he prayed it at some stage in the wilderness and it might well have been Marah: "Relent, LORD! How long will it be? Satisfy us in the morning with your unfailing love, that we may sing for joy and be glad all our days. Make us glad for as many days as you have afflicted us, for as many years as we have seen trouble. May your deeds be shown to your servants, your splendour to their children."[3]

During the twenty-one years that Jane spent in a wheelchair, I prayed these words regularly. It made the bitter waters sweet with hope that God would answer this powerful prayer that echoed the cry of my heart. God answered Moses' prayer by showing him a piece of wood. When he threw it into the waters, they became sweet. As wood and water do not react together chemically, this was a miracle.

Today, scholars identify the site of Marah as most likely being the oasis of Ain Hawarah, some seventy-five kilometres southeast of Suez on the traditional route to Mount Sinai. Its spring gives brackish water because of salts in the surrounding soil.[4]

Nevertheless, God sweetened the waters miraculously for a time, so that the Israelites could drink it. When, like Moses, we

---

3 Psalm 90:13-16 (NIV)

4 *Wycliffe Bible Encyclopedia Volume Two*, Chicago, Moody Press, 1975, p.1076

cry out to God in the midst of the bitter waters of life, he will spotlight the wood: the cross on which Jesus died.

The Cross Sweetens Life's Bitter Waters

Jesus bore our bitterness and sorrows on that wooden cross. If ever there were bitter injustice and cruelty, it was at Calvary where humankind crucified the Son of God. It was not fair. It was unjust. It was despicable. It was murder. He who was perfect died for our sin. Jesus drank the bitter waters of Calvary to the full, that he might make the bitter waters of our lives sweet.

When we view life's circumstances through the eyes of the cross, injustice, pain, and bitterness fade in the light of what Jesus endured for us. When we are tempted to feel resentful or complain, one look at the cross can stop those seeds growing in our hearts. Suffering greater bitterness than any of us will ever experience, Jesus knows what it is like, and thus has compassion for us.

In those times when life forces us to drink its bitter waters, we should lay our complaints down at the cross and worship the Lord. He will make the waters sweet, even if the circumstances do not change immediately.

Years and years of multiple sclerosis made life bitter for Jane and me. We lost much freedom and endured great hardship. And when Jane passed away, that bitter flavour intensified. At that time, some profound words of the apostle Paul challenged me: "I consider everything a loss because of the surpassing worth of knowing Christ Jesus my Lord, for whose sake I have lost all things. I consider them garbage, that I may gain Christ."[5]

I realised that the bitter waters did not matter – I had gained a knowledge of Jesus that surpassed all that had been lost. God gradually restored me, assured me of Jane's bliss in heaven, and brought Greta into my life. The sour taste of death and disappointment turned to sweetness in my soul. He makes all things beautiful in his time.

King David of Israel tasted bitter waters in his life. Despite great military success, he was pursued as an outlaw by the incumbent King Saul, committed adultery with Bathsheba later in life, arranged the murder of her husband, suffered the loss of their baby, experienced rape, murder, and betrayal within his family, and saw Israel judged because of his prideful taking of a census. Others forced some of these bitter experiences on him and some were due to his own foolish decisions. Yet he repented and sought forgiveness from God, who began to sweeten the waters.

The very site where the angel of death stood, poised to wipe out Jerusalem due to the census, became the site where the temple would be built. The very person who would build the temple was Solomon, the child born to David and Bathsheba after their first died. Towards the end of his life, when he dedicated a large amount of material for the construction of the temple, David composed a song for the dedication ceremony. A line of the song says, "For his anger lasts only a moment, but his favour lasts a lifetime! Weeping may last through the night, but joy comes with the morning."[6] That is what happens when

5 Philippians 3:8 (NIV)
6 Psalm 30:5

God makes the bitter waters of our lives sweet again.

A Tragedy

I came to Christ through the ministry of the Navigators at Canterbury University in Christchurch, New Zealand. I am forever grateful to them, and the grounding in God's word they gave me. The founder of the Navigators, Dawson Trotman, had a vision to make not mere converts but disciples who could make other disciples. Yet in 1956, an accident cut his life tragically short at age fifty, when he drowned rescuing a young woman while water-skiing in Schroon Lake, New York.

Here is one account of the incident:

> The bitter news of Trotman's drowning swept like cold wind across the lake to the shoreline. Eyewitnesses tell of the profound anxiety, the tears, the helpless disbelief in the faces of those who now looked out across the deep blue water. Everyone's face except one – Lila Trotman, Dawson's widow. As she suddenly walked upon the scene a close friend shouted, "Oh, Lila ... He's gone. Dawson's gone!" To that, she replied in calm assurance the words of Psalm 115:3, "But our God is in the heavens; He does whatever He pleases." All of the anguish, the sudden loneliness that normally consumes and cripples those who survive, did not invade that woman's heart. Instead, she leaned hard upon her sovereign Lord.[7]

---

7 www.sermonillustrations.com/a-z/t/tragedy.htm, accessed 10/1/14

If, when life sends us bitter waters, we lean upon God and gaze at the cross of Christ, we will not only cope but we will receive a revelation of God's ability to transform the worst of circumstances into something good.

It was at Marah, the place of healing of the waters, that God revealed his name YHWH-Rapha[8] to the Israelites. It means I am (the eternally unchanging one) who heals you. Moses, records, "'I am the LORD [YHWH in Hebrew] who heals you.' The Israelites travelled on to the oasis of Elim, where they found twelve springs and seventy palm trees. They camped there beside the water."[9]

He is the God who heals the bitter waters and after every Marah there is always an Elim. Not only does he make the bitter waters sweet, but he turns our losses to gain.

8 YHWH is pronounced Yahweh.

9 Exodus 15:26c-27

chapter seven

TURNING LOSS TO GAIN

It is one of the most beloved psalms. During the three thousand years since Israel's King David wrote Psalm 23, countless people have taken great comfort from its verses.

> The LORD is my shepherd, I lack nothing.
> He makes me lie down in green pastures,
> He leads me beside quiet waters, he refreshes my soul.
> He guides me along the right paths for his name's sake.
> Even though I walk through the darkest valley,
> I will fear no evil, for you are with me;
> your rod and your staff, they comfort me.
> You prepare a table before me in the presence of
> my enemies.
> You anoint my head with oil; my cup overflows.
> Surely your goodness and love will follow me all the
> days of my life,
> And I will dwell in the house of the LORD forever.[1]

---

1 Psalm 23 (NIV)

After Jane passed away, I read and re-read these words, memorising them, so that when despair would sometimes envelope me in the night, I could quote them. They became an antidote to the pain gnawing at my soul. Then one day, the Holy Spirit said to me, "Read it no longer as a pastoral psalm of comfort but as a prophetic psalm of promise." As I studied the words again, I saw that each verse is a doorway to the next and that the complete psalm is an unfolding journey into greater hope. Readers of the psalm love what the first verses promise to those who make the Lord their shepherd: no lack, green pastures, still waters, and restored souls. Verse three then states that, "He guides me along the right paths for his name's sake." This is so symptomatic of most people's early Christian experience. When we come to faith in Christ, this wonderful new relationship with our Shepherd-King restores our sin-ravaged souls, lifting the heavy load of our transgression from us. We feel refreshed. Life seems brighter. We are at rest. Peace and provision find us.

Filled with such knowledge of God's goodness, we boldly declare that we will follow him wherever he leads us and commit ourselves to his paths of righteousness. Yes, the first few verses of David's psalm are soothing and easy to read. Then the words change tone abruptly: "Even though I walk through the valley of the shadow of death, I will fear no evil, for you are with me. Your rod and your staff, they comfort me." As we begin our journey from the lush plain of green pastures and still waters, and stride out onto God's true paths, we may discover that there will be times when those very paths take us into the valley of the shadow of death. We may protest that we did not sign up for such a thing, but eventually, every true follower of Christ will pass through such a valley or valleys.

The valley of the shadow of death is one of loss. The loss may be literal, as in the death of a loved one or figurative, as in the death of some dream for the future, the demise of a business, a broken relationship, deteriorating health and so on. As death casts its shadow over us, grief may then invade our souls.

Coping in the Valley

We then have a choice. Like the Israelites at Marah, we can choose to complain and become embittered. Some who find themselves in such a valley become angry at God, asking how he could ever let them face such loss and why he did not spare them from it. Alternatively, we can choose to trust. For something good awaits us on the other side of the valley. How we navigate the valley of the shadow of death will determine whether we stay trapped there or whether we emerge from it. The key is to fear no evil. God works all things together for good, even death. He brings gain out of loss. Often in such a valley, the devil will entice us to fear the worst, and to think that we will never recover from it. That is evil, and it is vital not to fear it or yield to the lie – not easy when our pain may be screaming otherwise. Here, clinging to our trust in God's goodness, unmoved by the seeming evidence that shouts the opposite, we take one tentative step after another until our stride becomes strong. Light begins to dawn in that dark valley.

"The path of the righteous," explains the Bible, "is like the light of dawn, which shines brighter and brighter until full day."[2]

---

[2] Proverbs 4:18 (RSV)

As we walk in faith and not fear, we discover that our Shepherd's rod of protection and correction, and his staff of comfort, will assist us. For Middle Eastern shepherds, their rod and staff were vital pieces of equipment. They used the rod to strike predators that might attack the flock, and to discipline wayward sheep for their own safety. The staff, with a hook at one end, not only helped the shepherd support himself on rough terrain, but was also used to guide the sheep along the right path and, at times, rescue them if they had fallen into a hole or crevice. Additionally, the shepherd would use the staff to draw the sheep closer to himself for protection, warmth, or to examine their condition.

Jesus is not only the shepherd of green pastures and still waters, but he is also the shepherd of the valley. There, as we walk in simple trust, he will protect us, correct us when needed, and draw us to himself – all the time keeping us on the right path. The words *you are with me* speak of this constant presence. If we hold onto God in the valley of the shadow of death, then we will discover that, waiting on the other side of it, are things so wonderful that they will make the valley seem a distant memory.

After the Valley

"You prepare a table before me in the presence of my enemies," declares verse five. "You anoint my head with oil; my cup overflows." This is a beautiful picture of Middle Eastern hospitality. My paternal and maternal grandparents were born in Lebanon, emigrating from their home village of Bsharri in the northern Lebanese mountains to New Zealand, at the turn of the last century. Bsharri locals are renowned across the northern region for their wonderful hospitality. My Kiwi-born parents grew up steeped in this. I remember my mother preparing all sorts of delicious food days out from a special family gathering. On the day, the table was bourgeoning with dish after dish of savoury Lebanese food. It was the same when it came to dessert. No Middle Eastern table has mere bread and water; rather, it is crammed with delectable treats. When God prepares a table for those who have travelled the painful route of the valley of the shadow of death, it is a feast. He forces our enemies of death, loss, sickness, trouble, anxiety or fear to watch, as we feast on his goodness and provision.

Job was a man who walked through a deep, dark valley of death when he lost all his children and possessions. When his three closest friends came to comfort him, they erroneously accused him of committing some sin that had attracted God's judgment. Beware the accuser in the valley of loss. Some loss is indeed our own fault, and we need to repent of what caused it. However, other loss is beyond our control, and we must resist the guilt that the devil's voice of accusation will bring: "If only you had tried harder; if you had done more, if you had not said what you said …" One of Job's friends did, nevertheless, say something that was true: "He [God] is wooing you from the jaws of distress to a spacious place free from restriction, to the comfort of your table laden with choice food."[3] That is what our great Shepherd does when we trust him in the valley of loss. He turns our loss to gain.

Not only do we feast, but he also anoints our heads with oil, and our cup overflows. This anointing oil was not that used for commissioning priests and kings. Rather, a good host would provide olive oil for his guest's hair. It was the favoured hair

3 Job 36:16 (NIV)

product of the day, and in case we think that putting olive oil in our hair to make it shine is strange, the waxes, gels, and sprays we use today may well have repulsed the ancients! Once, when defending a woman from a Pharisee's criticism because she anointed his feet with perfume, Jesus explained to his host, "You neglected the courtesy of olive oil to anoint my head, but she has anointed my feet with rare perfume."[4] In a hospitality context, the phrase *you anoint my head with oil* thus represents favour. If your host favoured you, he would give you oil for your head.

In a shepherding context, the oil is medicinal. Shepherds carried a horn of oil, from which they would pour drops onto their sheep's head. Gradually the oil would work its way through the wool and kill the pests and parasites that irritated the sheep, much like modern flea treatments for pets. Perhaps King David, having been both a shepherd of the flock and a king who entertained many guests, had both meanings in mind when he penned these words. Our God will give us supernatural peace of mind as we journey through the valley, freeing us from the irritants that may trouble us, and grant us favour with him. When we have favour with God, we will also have favour with people, for they are attracted to one who has walked through the valley of the shadow of death and maintained a sweetness of soul by clinging to God. People will listen to their words for they will be credible.

Overflow

And our cup will overflow. This means that we will have more than enough for our needs, and thus represents provision. We

---

4 Luke 7:46

will not only eat his abundance while our enemies look on, but God will anoint us with favour and provision. What lies on the other side of the valley of the shadow of death? Feasting, favour and provision. Our faith will have grown and we will have new confidence in God's faithfulness and goodness, declaring that, "Surely goodness and love will follow me all the days of my life, and I will dwell in the house of the Lord forever." *The valley brings the surely.* Having seen God's faithfulness in the dark times, we know without doubt that his goodness will follow in all places and at all times, and even if we encounter further valleys, his goodness and mercy will pursue us there. Having faced death and loss, and looked upwards to him, we are filled with a confidence that there is something that lies beyond the grave. We know that, by his amazing grace, we will one day dwell in God's house forever. Like Jeremiah the prophet, we can say, "I will never forget this awful time, as I grieve over my loss. Yet I still dare to hope when I remember this: The faithful love of the LORD never ends! His mercies never cease. Great is his faithfulness; his mercies begin afresh each morning."[5]

Every valley in the Bible has a positive counterpoint. God turns the valley of the shadow of death into a place of feasting, favour, and provision, the valley of trouble into a gateway of hope,[6] the valley of weeping into a place of refreshing,[7] and the valley of dead, dry bones into a place of resurrection life.[8] He turns our losses to gain. There is life beyond death for the living, and we can recover.

---

5 Lamentations 3:20-23
6 See Hosea 2:15
7 See Psalm 84:6
8 See Ezekiel 37:1-10

chapter eight

WHAT ABOUT HEALING?

For twenty-five years, I prayed expectantly that God would heal Jane from multiple sclerosis. Yet it did not happen in the way I anticipated. And I am not alone. While there are growing reports of extraordinary healings throughout the world today, some wonder why their prayers for healing appear to go unanswered. When Jane passed away, I accepted it as a mystery; trusting that, over time, the Lord would give me some answers, and even if I did not get all of them until eternity, that would be alright.

However, I was determined to form my theology on healing from the Bible and not my circumstances, so I made the decision to continue to pray for the sick whenever opportunity arose, and to train others to do it as well. Over time, understanding of the area of divine healing came, and while not having all the answers to this complex area, I now have more than at the time of Jane's death.

Before we continue to explore this further, it would be helpful to know where sickness came from in the first place.

The Origin of Sickness

When God created the earth and placed Adam and Eve in the Garden of Eden, there was no sickness whatsoever. "Then God looked over all he had made," records the Bible, "and he saw that it was very good!"[1] If disease had been present from the beginning of creation, then this statement could not be true. Something happened that introduced disease into the world. That 'something' was what theologians term, *the fall.* When Adam and Eve rebelled against God, the earth came under a curse and death gripped creation.[2]

Some previously beneficial microbes altered genetically over time and became harmful and disease-producing. Further, genetic deterioration in the human race also brought disease. Today, we know that numerous diseases are due to faulty genes. Adam and Eve, designed by God to live forever, would have been genetically perfect at the beginning. The fall introduced a genetic deterioration in them and their descendants, albeit gradual.

The Bible records Adam as living for 930 years, a lifespan unimaginable today.[3] However, this is no surprise for a being created genetically perfect and susceptible to only gradual decline. Adam's descendants also lived very long lives, but after the Great Flood, reduction of life span accelerated.[4]

Noah lived 600 years, and by the time of Abraham, longevity

---

1 Genesis 1:31

2 See Genesis 3

3 Many ancient cultures have legends stating that before the Great Flood, kings (and presumably others) lived very long lives, but after the flood, their lifespans were shorter.

4 See Genesis 11: 10-32 for this dramatic post-flood decline in lifespan.

had reduced to 200 plus years. In Moses' time, average life expectancy was 120 years or less, much as it is today.

The Bible promises a future resurrection, when believers will receive perfect glorified bodies, and once more live forever, free from all sickness, aging, and decline.[5]

Secondly, the fall also brought another agent of sickness into play. After Satan deceived Adam and Eve into sin, they forfeited the right to rule planet earth to him. Satan became overlord of the earth and began to oppress humanity. When tempting Jesus to sin, the devil showed him all the kingdoms of the world and promised them to Jesus if he would bow down and worship him. "I will give you all their authority and splendour;" he assured Jesus, "it has been given to me, and I can give it to anyone I want to."[6] Jesus did not dispute this assertion. Adam and Eve had unwittingly given Satan and his demons authority to rule and oppress their descendants.

For example, when afflicting God's servant Job, Satan sent natural disasters and bandits to bring ruin, devastating loss, and death to Job's family. Finally, he afflicted Job himself with a terrible infection that produced painful sores all over his body.[7] After healing a woman on the Sabbath from an afflicting spirit that caused her to be bent double, Jesus explained to some indignant Pharisees, "Should not this woman, a daughter of Abraham, whom Satan has kept bound for eighteen long years, be set free on the Sabbath day from what bound her?"[8]

---

5 See chapter 12 for more detail.
6 Luke 4:6 (NIV)
7 See Job 1:13-19 and 2:7
8 Luke 13:16 (NIV)

In his ministry, Jesus healed numbers of people from sickness by casting out evil spirits causing the affliction. Not all sickness is demonic, but some clearly is. The good news is that through his sacrificial death on the cross, Jesus broke Satan's rule over the earth and the human race. The Kingdom of God is now upon the earth – not yet fully, but nevertheless here. With the coming of the Kingdom and the restoration of the right to rule planet earth restored to the second Adam, Jesus, and the second Eve, the Church, people can be set free from sickness, regardless of the cause.

Summarising Jesus' ministry, the apostle Peter explained, "You know that God anointed Jesus of Nazareth with the Holy Spirit and with power. Then Jesus went around doing good and healing all who were oppressed by the devil, for God was with him."[9]

Poor lifestyle is a third cause of sickness. If we disregard rules for healthy living such as a good diet, reasonable amounts of exercise, and proper rest, then we may suffer physically. Violation of these rules, for example, has contributed to the current global epidemic of obesity, bringing illness to many. It is one thing to experience divine healing; it is another to live in divine health. God expects us to take good care of our bodies, which are temples of the Holy Spirit. If either medicine or a miracle heals a person, it is simple wisdom to make lifestyle adjustments in order to remain healthy.

A fourth reason for sickness is God himself. There are rare times when God does send illness as a judgment for wrongdoing. For example, Miriam was stricken with leprosy for seven days

---

9 Acts 10:38

when she rebelled against her brother Moses' leadership.[10] An angel from God struck King Herod with a fatal parasitic disease because he accepted worship as a god from his people.[11] Jesus threatened to throw a false prophet on her sickbed for teaching that sexual immorality and idolatry were permissible for Christians.[12] These are all very serious cases and we must not take them to mean that God will afflict us with sickness for any old sin. I believe that the vast majority of sickness – probably ninety-nine percent – is due to the first three causes.

Healing is Available

Concerning the crowds that followed Jesus wherever he went, Luke the physician records, "They had come to hear him *and* to be healed of their diseases; and those troubled by evil spirits were healed."[13] The 'and' has been missing from much of the modern church. Today, at least in the West, people come largely to church to hear inspiring songs of worship, an uplifting sermon, and perhaps a testimony or two. The 'and' needs to be restored. As one pastor put it, "We need to get back to more show and tell." Jesus never meant us to proclaim the gospel of the Kingdom in word only. When commissioning seventy-two of his disciples to preach the gospel, he told them, "Heal the sick, and tell them, 'The Kingdom of God is near you now.'"[14] The disciples were to not only proclaim the Kingdom of God, but also demonstrate it. Explaining to the Corinthians his strategy of reaching them with the gospel, the apostle Paul stated, "My

10 See Numbers 12:9-11
11 See Acts 12:23
12 See Revelation 2:20-22
13 Luke 6:18
14 Luke 10:9

message and my preaching were not with wise and persuasive words, but with a demonstration of the Spirit's power, so that your faith might not rest on human wisdom, but on God's power."[15]

Jesus regarded healing as displaying God's compassion and mercy to meet human need, and as a sign pointing to salvation and forgiveness of sins.[16] The early church saw healing as the premiere sign pointing to Christ and validating the gospel. When the Jewish High Council warned them to stop preaching in the name of Jesus, the apostles, together with the church, prayed, "O Lord, hear their threats, and give us, your servants, great boldness in preaching your word. Stretch out your hand with healing power; may miraculous signs and wonders be done through the name of your holy servant Jesus."[17] We see from this that the early church prioritised the ministry of preaching and healing.

I sometimes hear people praying, "Lord, if it is your will, heal this person." That kind of prayer generally does not heal anyone. It is God's will to heal. The extensive healing ministry of Jesus provides conclusive evidence of God's attitude to sickness. His nature is to heal. If this is true, and it is, then we must ask why healing eludes some people.

---

15 1 Corinthians 2:4-5 (NIV)

16 See Luke 7:11-15; 5:17-25

17 Acts 4:29-30

Hindrances to Healing

One reason some do not receive healing is due to unbelief or doubt, either individually or corporately. When Jesus was dishonoured in his home town of Nazareth, and the townspeople refused to believe in him, the Bible states, "And he did not do many miracles there because of their lack of faith."[18]

Most of us do not have a problem with unbelief – the refusal to believe – but we may have a problem with doubt. We might believe that God heals, but then doubt that he would in our case; or we might pray for someone else to be healed, but doubt that anything will happen. "I tell you the truth," promised Jesus, "you can say to this mountain, 'May you be lifted up and thrown into the sea,' and it will happen. But you must really believe it will happen and have no doubt in your heart."[19]

Greta and I once ministered at a large church, and though thrilled to see the powerful moving of the Holy Spirit upon the people, we were surprised that very few healings took place. When we asked the Lord about this in prayer, we sensed that a stronghold of doubt in the church was inhibiting healing. On discussing this with the pastor, he admitted that he had done a Bible College thesis on healing, in which he posited that God does heal, but not all the time. Thus, every time he prayed for someone, he doubted that anything would happen. We encouraged him to consider changing his theology! To his credit, he later confessed in front of the leaders of the church, and prayed that God would release his healing power. Some months later, he wrote to say that they had seen scores of documented healings in the church.

---

18 Matthew 13:58 (NIV)

19 Mark 11:23

A second blockage to healing is unforgiveness. This hinders God's ability to show us mercy and grace because we are not showing it to others. "If you forgive those who sin against you, your heavenly Father will forgive you." Jesus taught, "But if you refuse to forgive others, your Father will not forgive your sins."[20] We may feel that to forgive the offender is to forego justice. In reality, our lack of forgiveness keeps us in a prison of bondage, which may include illness. By forgiving, we show mercy and thus God will show mercy to us, and bring justice if needed. We once met a woman who had, for many years, suffered pelvic pain from childbirth. Though prayed for numerous times, she had never experienced full healing. On discovering that she held a grudge against the gynecologist who had attended her, we encouraged her to forgive him. She did so, and when prayed for, reported complete freedom from pain for the first time.

A further reason some are not healed may be due to them being cursed. In these cases, the person needs deliverance before healing can occur. In one of the schools of the supernatural that Greta and I conduct in a number of nations, a student prayed for a woman on crutches. Nothing happened so she asked us to intervene.

We discovered that the woman had broken her foot some four months before, but the fracture had not healed, which puzzled the doctors. On questioning her further, we discovered that she had been on a missions trip to Africa when the injury happened and that she had noticed a woman glaring at her in a very dark way. Discerning that this woman had cursed her, we broke the curse in Jesus' name, rebuked an afflicting spirit, and then prayed for her foot. We then asked her to test her foot carefully, but she ignored us and began jumping up and down

---

20 Matthew 6:14-15

on it without any pain. A little while later, she emailed us to say that an X-ray had shown complete healing of the fracture.

In a similar way, involvement in occult practices such as witchcraft, astrology, fortune telling, séances, or membership in lodges that have occultic undertones such as freemasonry or the druids lodge, can all hinder healing. The person needs to repent of these and then any demonisation dealt with, before prayer for healing. Likewise, when the same sickness is prevalent in a number of family members, it usually indicates that a hereditary spirit of sickness is at work in the family line. Once renounced, this can be broken off and then healing can take place.

According to the apostle Paul, consistent divisiveness, and dishonouring the body of Christ while partaking in communion, also hinders the release of healing: "For if you eat the bread or drink the cup without honouring the body of Christ, you are eating and drinking God's judgment upon yourself. That is why many of you are weak and sick and some have even died. But if we would examine ourselves, we would not be judged by God in this way."[21]

These are some of the Biblical reasons that may prevent healing. Healing is perfectly available because of the cross of Christ, but, at times, imperfectly ministered or received. We do not yet see everyone who receives prayer, healed. I have hope that will change. Sometimes, people appear to do everything right in believing for healing, and still it does not come and perhaps the person may even die. It is then that we need to accept the mysterious in our walk with God, and bow to him. We should not, however, reduce our theology about healing to the level of our circumstances, or doubt God's goodness or

---

[21] 1 Corinthians 11:29-31

willingness to heal.

An Often Unused Key to Healing the Sick

Once, when Jesus asked his disciples who they thought he was, Simon Peter answered, "You are the Messiah, the Son of the living God." Jesus replied, "You are blessed, Simon son of John, because my Father in heaven has revealed this to you … and I will give you the keys of the Kingdom of Heaven. Whatever you forbid on earth will be forbidden in heaven, and whatever you permit on earth will be permitted in heaven."[22]

Keys open and shut doors and thus represent authority. If someone gives you the keys to their house, they are giving you the authority to enter it. If we have a revelation of who Jesus is, he gives us keys of authority. However, we often do not use the keys properly. For example, imagine that I ask to borrow your car and you walk me to the vehicle and hand over the keys. Then suppose I hesitate to unlock the car, hand back the keys, and request that you open the door instead. You would think it very strange indeed. Yet when we pray, "Lord Jesus, please heal this person," this is exactly what we are doing. We are asking him to do it. However, Jesus has given us the keys and told us to heal the sick. When instead we move from prayer to command and say, "Be healed in Jesus' name!" and believe it will happen, we are using the keys. I have rarely seen many healed when only prayer has been offered. It takes command as well. We are to not only pray it, but we are to say it.

---

22 Matthew 16:16-17, 19

Peter certainly used the keys of authority that Jesus gave him. Once, when some believers asked him to pray for a recently deceased woman named Tabitha, Peter demonstrated correct use of those keys. The Bible records, "But Peter asked them all to leave the room; then he knelt and prayed. Turning to the body he said, "Get up, Tabitha." And she opened her eyes! When she saw Peter, she sat up!"[23] It was right to pray. Prayer is an expression of humble dependence on the Lord and invites the Holy Spirit into the situation. However, nothing happened to Tabitha when Peter simply prayed. Only when he turned to the body and commanded her to wake up did something happen.

The apostle Paul followed a similar approach. After a violent storm shipwrecked Paul and his fellow survivors on the island of Malta, Publius the governor showed them generous hospitality for some days. Paul then healed the governor's father who was ill in bed from fever and dysentery. "Paul went into see him," records the Bible, "and after prayer, placed his hands on him and healed him. Then all the other sick people on the island came and were healed."[24] This method of prayer and command is not a formula, but a principle. Jesus, who lived in a daily prayer relationship with his Father, commanded the sick to be healed, and authorises believers to do the same.

When we have the same attitude as God towards sickness, we will see more people healed. "A man with leprosy came and knelt in front of Jesus, begging to be healed," records the gospel of Mark. "If you are willing, you can heal me and make me clean," he said. Moved with compassion, Jesus reached out and touched him. "I am willing," he said. "Be healed!" Instantly

---

23 Acts 9:40

24 Acts 28:8 (NIV), 9 (NLT)

the leprosy disappeared, and the man was healed."[25] Jesus left the man in no doubt that he wanted to heal him. His response reveals God's heart to heal. It is interesting to note that the Greek word for 'compassion' in this verse can also be translated as 'anger', various bibles rendering it differently. This is not a conflict. Both are true. The Lord has compassion for the sick and anger towards sickness. This is what we should feel as well. Then his power will flow as we use the keys he has given us.

And even if we appear to lose some battles, and those we pray for do not improve and eventually die, as Jane did, we can be assured that death is no defeat for the believer. As we shall see in the remainder of this book, to die is gain.

---

25 Mark 1:40-42

PART 2

LIFE BEYOND DEATH FOR THE DEPARTED

chapter nine

WHAT HAPPENS WHEN YOU DIE?

From the time Adam and Eve first sinned many millennia ago, every human being has faced death. "No one can live forever; all will die," records the psalmist, "No one can escape the power of the grave."[1] God never intended people to die; rather, he created us to live forever. When the first man and woman sinned, they forfeited the right to everlasting life. God declared to them, "You were made from dust, and to dust you will return."[2] Death has overshadowed the human race ever since. "None of us can hold back our spirit from departing," states the Bible. "None of us has the power to prevent the day of our death. There is no escaping that obligation, that dark battle."[3]

---

1 Psalm 89:48
2 Genesis 3:19
3 Ecclesiastes 8:8

Ever since the first humans began to bury their dead, one great question has puzzled humankind: is there life after death? Surveys suggest that more than seventy percent of people worldwide believe there is an afterlife. They may have different ideas of what that afterlife looks like, but they believe death is not the end. This is because God has wired us to believe that there is more than this present life. Solomon wrote, "He has planted eternity in the human heart."[4]

While medical science has many stories of people who have died, been resuscitated, and reported seeing an afterlife, it is to the Bible that we must turn for conclusive proof concerning life after death. The Bible has stood the test of time for two thousand years and longer. Men have suppressed and burned it, the devil has fought it, but the word of God remains the top bestselling book in the world. It is God's blueprint for humankind.

Understanding Death

"Each person is destined to die once," records the book of Hebrews, "and after that comes judgment."[5] Our destiny is to die. Today, people try all kinds of ways to prolong life. Some even go as far as having their bodies cryogenically frozen in the hope that, sometime in the future, science will be able to resurrect them. But it will not happen. Moses, writing down the oral traditions passed from Adam to successive generations, records God as saying of Adam, "'He must not be allowed to reach out his hand and take also from the tree of life and eat, and live forever.' So the LORD God banished him from the

---

4 Ecclesiastes 3:11

5 Hebrews 9:27

Garden of Eden to work the ground from which he had been taken. After he drove the man out, he placed on the east side of the Garden of Eden cherubim and a flaming sword flashing back and forth to guard the way to the tree of life."[6]

Fearing that humankind would live forever in a fallen, sinful state, God barred the way to the tree of life with a flaming sword. Though Eden is long gone, that sword still exists today. God will not permit any way back to the tree of life by human effort. Only in Christ can we eat of that tree again and live forever. "To everyone who is victorious," declares Jesus, "I will give fruit from the tree of life in the paradise of God."[7]

Note that our destiny is to die only once. There is no reincarnation. This belief gives false hope that a person can come back to earth in some other form after their death. One well-known actor famously declared that she was an orphan raised by elephants in a former life![8] In parts of Asia, millions live in abject poverty. Many in their community who could help them claim that the poor are merely receiving punishment for sins committed in a former life and have thus been reincarnated in that state. It is believed that by suffering they might attain to a higher form next time round. This devilish lie offers no hope to anyone. The Bible simply declares that we die once, and after that comes judgment; a judgment to determine our position in eternity. We will explore the nature of this judgment in later chapters.

What exactly happens at death? James, the brother of Jesus,

---

6 Genesis 3:22-24 (NIV)
7 Revelation 2:7
8 http://books.google.co.nzbooks?id=hdhxSK2b30gC&pg=PA91&lpg=PA91&dq accessed 4/9/2014

says, "As the body without the spirit is dead, so faith without deeds is dead."[9] While he is emphasising faith, James indirectly makes an interesting statement about death – the body is dead without a spirit. Human beings, made in the image of the triune God (Father, Son, and Holy Spirit) comprise body, soul, and spirit.[10] While the body is physical world conscious, the spirit is spiritual world conscious. The soul consists of mind, emotions, and will, and interacts with both body and spirit.

The spirit and soul transcend the mortal body and live on after death. Medical science is now verifying this with numbers of resuscitated people reporting near-death experiences where they claim that their spirits left their bodies. Thus, death is the departure of the spirit and soul – our inner being – from the body. For simplicity sake, I will refer to the spirit and soul as just the spirit from this point on. Now where does the spirit go? "For then the dust [body] will return to the earth," writes Solomon, "and the spirit will return to God who gave it."[11] The spirit returns to God for an immediate judgment (called 'particular judgment' by theologians) to determine where it will then be sent. (This is in contrast to the last and full judgment that awaits the end of time.)

There are two possible destinations depending on whether a person is a believer or a non-believer in Jesus Christ.

---

9 James 2:26 (NIV)
10 See 1 Thessalonians 5:23
11 Ecclesiastes 12:7

Death for a Believer

Believers are those who believe that Jesus Christ is God, died on the cross for their sins, and rose again. They have believed in, and received, him. "But to all who believed him and accepted him," writes the apostle John, "he gave the right to become children of God."[12] As with the rest of humankind, a believer's body goes to the grave at death, but their spirit goes to heaven, the home of God's children, where Christ also dwells. "We are fully confident," states the apostle Paul, "and we would rather be away from these earthly bodies, for then we will be at home with the Lord."[13]

In one of the most hope-filled statements on death in the Bible, Paul says, "For to me, to live is Christ and to die is gain ... I am torn between the two: I desire to depart and be with Christ, which is better by far; but it is more necessary for you that I remain in the body."[14]

Luke, narrating the story of Stephen, the first martyr of the Christian church, records, "As they stoned him, Stephen prayed, 'Lord Jesus, receive my spirit.'"[15] Both Paul and Stephen expected their spirits would go to be with the Lord at death, and would be conscious in heaven.

---

12 John 1:12
13 2 Corinthians 5:8
14 Philippians 1:21 (NKJV), 23-24 (NIV)
15 Acts 7:59

No Soul Sleep

Some Christians believe mistakenly that the spirit goes to sleep, and is not conscious until Jesus raises the deceased person's body from the dead when he returns. They base this belief largely on scriptures where sleep is used as a metaphor for death. For example, Paul writes to believers grieving the death of loved ones, "We do not want you to be uninformed about those who sleep in death, so that you do not grieve like the rest of mankind, who have no hope."[16] Some take this to mean that the spirit rests in an unconscious state until the resurrection of the body. However, Paul is merely using the symbol of sleep to describe death, in order to comfort those who were unsure they would see their deceased loved ones again. As wakening follows sleep, so resurrection follows death.

The Bible is clear that, after death, the spirit remains conscious. Isaiah, when prophesying about the demise of the king of Babylon, says, "In the place of the dead there is excitement over your arrival. The spirits of world leaders and mighty kings long dead stand up to see you. With one voice they all cry out, 'Now you are as weak as we are!'"[17] If these dead people were in a state of soul sleep, they would feel no excitement, not be able to speak, and certainly would not stand to attention when the king of Babylon arrived.

Similarly, when the apostle John had a vision of heaven, he wrote, "I saw a vast crowd, too great to count, from every nation and tribe and people and language, standing in front of the

---

16 1 Thessalonians 4:13(NIV). See also 1 Corinthians 11:30 and 1 Corinthians 15:6, 18, 20, 51.

17 Isaiah 14:9-10

throne and before the Lamb. They were clothed in white robes ... and they were shouting with a great roar, 'Salvation comes from our God who sits on the throne and from the Lamb!'"[18] As this occurs before John's later vision of the bodily resurrection of the dead, it clearly refers to those who have died in Christ and who are now in heaven.

The writer to the Hebrews also provides evidence of consciousness of the spirit after death, when he says, "You have come to the spirits of the righteous ones in heaven who have now been made perfect."[19]

When a believer dies, his or her spirit goes to be with the Lord in heaven, and is not only conscious but enters a perfected state. The conclusive proof that there is no soul sleep is found in this statement of the apostle Paul's: "We would rather be away from these earthly bodies, for then we will be at home with the Lord."[20]

Spirit Bodies

If the dead are spirits without bodies in the afterlife, what form do they take? Are spirits nebulous clouds or wispy ghosts, or do they have a kind of bodily form? The Bible records many visions of heaven in which God, angels, and departed believers, though spirits, appear in human-like form. The prophet Ezekiel, describing his vision of God on his throne, writes, "On this throne high above was a figure whose appearance resembled a

18 See Revelation 7:9-10
19 Hebrews 12:23
20 2 Corinthians 5:8

man. From what appeared to be his waist up, he looked like gleaming amber, flickering like a fire. And from his waist down, he looked like a burning flame, shining with splendour."[21]

In a vision of the angel Gabriel, Daniel records, "Someone who looked like a man stood in front of me. And I heard a human voice calling out, 'Gabriel, tell this man the meaning of his vision.'"[22]

In visions of heaven the Lord has granted to many people, departed believers are seen as having a human-like form, even though they are spirits without bodies. It seems that their spirits have the same form as the bodies that once housed them. They wear robes. They walk, talk, sing, and smile. They await their resurrected physical bodies at the end of time, but have a spirit body suited to the temporary state they are in.

Visiting Heaven

Here is the testimony of a man who suffered a heart attack and stopped breathing:

> Next thing I remember was going through this dark passage. I didn't touch any of the walls. I emerged into an open field and was walking toward a big white wall which was very long. It had three steps leading up to a doorway in the wall. On a landing above the stairs sat a man clothed in a robe that was dazzling white and glowing. His face had a glowing

---

21 Ezekiel 1: 26-27
22 Daniel 8:15-16

radiance also. He was looking down into a big book, studying.

As I approached him, I felt a great reverence and I asked him, "Are you Jesus?"

He said, "No, you will find Jesus and your loved ones beyond that door." After he looked in his book he said, "You may go through."

And then I walked through the door and saw on the other side this beautiful, brilliantly lit city, reflecting what seemed to be the sun's rays. It was all made of gold, or some shiny metal, with domes and steeples in beautiful array, and the streets were shining, not quite like marble but made of something I had never seen before. There were many people dressed in glowing white robes with radiant faces. They looked beautiful. The air smelled so fresh. I have never smelled anything like it.

There was background music that was beautiful, heavenly music and I saw two figures walking towards me and I immediately recognised them. They were my mother and father; both had died years ago. My mother was an amputee and yet that leg was now restored! She was walking on two legs!

I said to my mother, "You and father are beautiful."

And they said to me, "You have the same radiance and you are also beautiful."

As we walked along together to find Jesus, I noticed there was one building larger than all the others. It looked like a football stadium with an open end to the building where a blinding light radiated from it. I tried to look up at the light but I couldn't. It was too brilliant. Many people seemed to be bowed in front of this building in adoration and prayer.

I said to my parents, "What is that?"

They said, "In there is God."

I will never forget it. I have never seen anything like it. We walked on, as they were taking me to see Jesus, and we passed many people. All of them were happy. I have never felt such a sense of wellbeing. As we approached the place where Jesus was, I suddenly felt this tremendous surge of electricity through my body as if someone had hit me in the chest. I had been restored to my former life! But I was not too happy to come back. However, I knew I had been sent back to tell others about this experience.[23]

Death for a Non-Believer

Non-believers are those who do not believe in God, or have rejected the grace of forgiveness he offers them in Christ, preferring to live independently from God. Like a believer, their bodies go to the grave, but their spirits go to a destination

23 Maurice Rawlings, *Beyond Death's Door*, Nashville, Thomas Nelson Publishers, 1978, p. 98

different from heaven. The New Testament uses the Greek word Hades to describe this place of the departed spirits of non-believers, while the Old Testament uses the Hebrew name Sheol. The English translation of the Bible simply uses the single term hell for both of the Greek and Hebrew words.

As mentioned before, Jesus once told a story about a rich man and a beggar who both died.[24] He was not commenting on whether riches or poverty determine whether you enter heaven or hell. Rather, it is a story about someone who leaves God out of his life. The rich man gave no thought for God, enjoyed the good life, and did not worry about helping anyone else, including the beggar, who finally succumbed to poverty and disease and passed away. Around the same time, the wealthy man died too.

The Bible records, "The time came when the beggar died and the angels carried him to Abraham's side. The rich man also died and was buried. In Hades, where he was in torment, he looked up and saw Abraham far away, with Lazarus by his side. So he called to him, 'Father Abraham, have pity on me and send Lazarus to dip the tip of his finger in water and cool my tongue, because I am in agony in this fire.'"[25]

Notice some things about this story: angels escort God's chosen into Paradise. That is a great comfort, as God ensures that the journey from this life to the next will be no lonely one. Secondly, Hades is a place of torment and agony. The rich man's spirit was conscious, felt pain, and cried out for mercy, but it was too late. Abraham replied, "Son, remember that in your lifetime you received your good things, while Lazarus received

---

24 See Luke 16:19-31
25 Luke 16:22-24 (NIV)

bad things, but now he is comforted here and you are in agony. And besides all this, between us and you a great chasm has been set in place, so that those who want to go from here to you cannot, nor can anyone cross over from there to us.'"[26]

In the movie, *What Dreams May Come,*[27] Robin Williams plays the hero Chris, who dies and goes to Paradise. Later his wife Annie, grief stricken by his loss and the previous death of their two children in a car accident, commits suicide and goes to hell. On discovering his deceased wife is in hell, Chris ventures into Hades, which is horrifically depicted in the movie with fire, torment, trapped souls, and every vile thing imaginable. Finally he locates his wife, rescues her, and eventually the pair ascend to Paradise. The film ends with them being reincarnated on earth and meeting again as children. Though the faulty theology is pure Hollywood, I remember the cinema falling deathly quiet and cold with fear as the hell scenes played on the screen.

The truth is Hades is unimaginably horrible. The deception is that it is possible to get out. Jesus made it clear that it is not.

Paradise in Hades?

Another thing to notice from Jesus' story, is that it seems that prior to Christ's death on the cross, people understood that Hades or Sheol was also the place of the departed spirits of believers. Though this is a debatable point among Christians, many believe that lower Sheol was a place of torment where the rich man found himself. Above a great gulf lay upper Sheol,

---

26 Luke 16:25-26 (NIV)

27 *What Dreams May Come*, ©1998, Universal Studios

called Abraham's Side or Paradise, a beautiful place of rest and joy. Here the spirits of Old Testament believers waited until the way into heaven was opened.

In the previously cited story of a medium conjuring up the spirit of Samuel for King Saul, something forbidden by God's word, the Lord permits Samuel to speak to Saul. The medium describes to Saul what she sees: "'I saw a spirit ascending out of the earth … an old man is coming up, and he *is* covered with a mantle.' And Saul perceived that it was Samuel."[28] The fact that Samuel ascended from beneath the earth, the traditional location for Sheol, seems to infer that Paradise before the cross was located in upper Sheol.[29]

Through his death on the cross, Jesus then opened the way into heaven for believers. Could this explain the unusual event recorded in the gospel of Matthew? "The bodies of many godly men and women who had died were raised from the dead," writes Matthew. "They left the cemetery after Jesus' resurrection, went into the holy city of Jerusalem, and appeared to many people."[30] While the Bible is silent on what happened to these resurrected believers after that, could they have been the first fruits of all those Old Testament saints who could now access heaven?

---

28 1 Samuel 28:13-14(NKJV)

29 Some may argue that Enoch (Genesis 5:24) and Elijah (2 Kings 2:11) were both taken bodily to heaven without dying, thus inferring that Old Testament saints went to heaven. They may well have a point. However other scriptures suggest that the saints went to Sheol, Enoch and Elijah being unusual cases, so the matter is open for debate.

30 Matthew 27:52-53

One thing is for certain – Paradise is now in heaven. The apostle Paul, commenting on his visitation into heaven, equates paradise and heaven thus, "I was caught up to the third heaven … I was caught up to paradise."[31]

Visiting Hell

Here is the story of a woman who had a cardiac arrest while undergoing surgery:

> I started to go down and down. It was horrific. I could see faces in pits, contorted with agony and pain. What made this downward journey terrifying were the lost souls I could see … I came into a room where I could smell sulphur and I saw a lake of fire and could feel the flames and heat from that fire. My thoughts were if I hit the bottom I would stay there forever – never-ending night and day for eternity, in that dreadful place where fear, pain and torment never stop.
>
> It was bad enough hearing the screams and seeing indescribable horrors, but then I saw my own father in that place. My father had been a good man and became very sick with cancer. The vicar came to see him and asked if he could pray but my father had refused any prayer or mention of Jesus. He wanted nothing to do with Him. Now as I looked at him, I knew he regretted that decision to turn his back

---

31 2 Corinthians 12:2, 4

> on Jesus; it was his free will choice, but with what devastating consequences.
>
> The heat was unbearable and I also knew there was nothing I could do to release my father from his 'chosen' destination. I was also terrified lest I should be dragged down and forced to stay there. In my desperation I cried out, "Oh God, please help me!'"
>
> At the moment of crying out to God, I heard another voice saying, "We have a heartbeat!''[32]

Sadly, though death is a glorious beginning for some, it will be a horrifying end for others, because the opportunity to be saved will be gone. Today there are many who gamble that there is nothing after death. They gamble that there is no God or no hell. Or if they believe in a heaven, they wager that surely they are not bad enough to be denied entry. Thus they are staking their eternal destination on a bet. That is a very foolish thing to do.

God is not indifferent to the death of any person. "Precious in the sight of the Lord is the death of his saints,"[33] records the psalmist. It is precious because God lovingly welcomes the believer into his presence. Equally, God tells Ezekiel the prophet, "I take no pleasure in the death of wicked people. I only want them to turn from their wicked ways so they can live."[34] It gives the Lord no joy to send a departed spirit to hell.

---

32 Richard Kent & Val Fotherby, *The Final Frontier*, London, Marshall Pickering, 1997, p.51

33 Psalm 116:15 (NKJV)

34 Ezekiel 33:11

We only have one life and that is why it must be lived well. And it must be lived for God.

In the next chapter, we will explore what heaven is like for the believers there already.

chapter ten

WHAT IS HEAVEN LIKE?

Colton Burpo went to heaven. Rushed into surgery with an appendix that had burst five days before, his prognosis was grim. Todd and Sonja Burpo, his parents, prayed desperately, alerting others from the church they pastored in the small town of Imperial, Nebraska, to do likewise. Miraculously, Colton, not yet four, survived, and slowly bounced back to normality.

Over the following months, little Colton began to reveal some startling things to his parents. He claimed that angels had sung to him and that he had seen Jesus. Then one day he told his mother that he had met his other sister. Sonja had miscarried a baby girl, but had never spoken of it with Colton. On questioning how he knew, Colton matter-of-factly announced that she had introduced herself to him in heaven and had given him lots of hugs!

Claiming to have also met Todd's grandfather, Colton pointed him out in an old photo of the man when he was younger, and did not recognise a picture of an elderly 'Pop', whom he had never met in real life.

Todd has since written a book, *Heaven is for Real*, which has become a New York Times bestseller, and been made into a movie of the same name.[1] This story has inspired hope in many worldwide. As already discussed in chapter three, Colton's experience is not unique; many others have also had similar encounters with heaven, not only now but throughout history. So what is heaven really like?

Organic and Inorganic Beauty

Speaking of heaven, the writer to the Hebrews says, "You have come to Mount Zion, to the city of the living God, the heavenly Jerusalem."[2] The City of God, the New Jerusalem, is the centrepiece of heaven. The city's beauty is more inorganic than organic. Foundations of precious stones, walls of jasper,[3] gates of giant pearls, and streets of gold so pure that it appears transparent, all contribute to its splendour.[4] Some think that these descriptions are merely symbolic, but I believe them to be real. Consider humankind's greatest buildings, both historical and modern. These have often comprised stone, gold, silver, marble, steel, glass, and concrete, and we marvel at their mineral and metal beauty.

---

1 Todd Burpo, *Heaven is for Real*, Nashville, Thomas Nelson, 2010. *Heaven is for Real* movie, ©2014, Columbia Pictures Industries Inc.

2 Hebrews 12:22 (NIV)

3 Although the term jasper is now restricted to mean opaque quartz, the jasper of antiquity was in many cases primarily green, often being compared to emeralds.

4 See Revelation 21

It is entirely reasonable that this is a reflection of things in heaven.[5]

On the other hand, many who have had visions of heaven also report that the city both contains, and is surrounded by, organic beauty. Verdant grass, beautiful trees, lush vegetation, crystal clear lakes, rivers and waterfalls, exquisite birds and friendly animals also appear to make up our heavenly home. Some have even described seeing their deceased pets! In other words, paradise is like earth, only infinitely better and perfect. While visions cannot speak with the same authority as the scriptures, they nevertheless may give us a glimpse of what that realm is like. The Bible reveals that there are a river, trees of life, and horses in heaven,[6] so it should come as no surprise that everything good we see on earth could be there, only in flawless form.

If God made humankind in his image, then it is plausible that he also made planet earth in the image of heaven, although that image has now been marred by the fall. Heaven is an inorganic and organic paradise. Everything is completely pure, perfect, delightful, and astonishing in its magnificence, as befits God's home. Colours are more vivid and varied than on earth, and the warmth of God's love pervades everything.

---

5 For example, when commenting on the Tabernacle of Moses, a design given by God to allow Israel to approach him, Hebrews 9:23 says, "That is why the Tabernacle and everything in it, which were copies of things in heaven, had to be purified by the blood of animals. But the real things in heaven had to be purified with far better sacrifices than the blood of animals." The Tabernacle was a copy of things in heaven so it is reasonable to assume that other things on earth are copies of things in heaven, albeit lesser copies.

6 See Revelation 6:1-8; 19:11 &14; 22:1-2.

In one vision of heaven the Lord gave me, I remember strolling through a forest of majestic trees and spreading ferns. What impacted me most was the fact that there were no dead leaves anywhere, and no musty smell of decaying vegetation. There is simply no death of any form in heaven.

Children in Heaven

Most people who have had visions of heaven, or near-death experiences, claim to have seen deceased loved ones looking younger than when they died on earth. The elderly on earth become young again in heaven. Their appearance is of someone in the absolute prime of adulthood, perhaps similar to Jesus when he started his ministry at age thirty, or Adam and Eve when God created them as fully-formed adults. Those who have had these visions rejoice to see the effects of earth's aging process rolled back in heaven. There, the spirits of the redeemed have been made perfect.

However, a number of others claim to have also seen children in heaven. One would think that if the aged become young again in heaven, surely those who die young would join them in adulthood?[7] It seems that this may not be so. My wife Greta relates a vision she once had:

> Jesus and I came to a beautiful waterfall with green grassy banks on either side of a river. Children played and laughed in the cascading water, while angels stood on the bank watching. I sensed that

---

7 I use these terms of age from an earthly viewpoint, because there is no aging in heaven.

they were taking care of the children.

To my surprise, a beautiful little girl with long blonde hair approached us, accompanied by her angel. Jesus had arranged this meeting. She said her name was Kelly. Born prematurely, she was a baby who had died of respiratory failure in the neonatal intensive care unit of Groote Schuur Hospital, the large teaching hospital where I had worked as a physiotherapist many years ago.

I had always remembered that event as if it had happened yesterday. I recalled the scene vividly: doctors, nurses, and myself all standing around her cubicle fighting to save her life. Even though this baby was a premmie, she had focused her big, blue bright eyes on me. They remained locked on mine in the midst of the feverish activity swirling around her tiny body. There was an unusually clear 'knowing' in her eyes, way beyond her age. My heart welled with love for her.

She now explained to me that Father had brought her straight home to heaven, and she was so happy and loved there. To see how blessed she was in that amazing place filled me with both joy and relief.

Could it be that a merciful heavenly Father allows precious children who have been aborted in the womb, miscarried, or who have died young, to enjoy their childhood in heaven?[8] Though premature death has robbed them of their destiny and purpose on earth, could it be that God is training them for their destiny in the new earth and heaven he will create? This is conjecture of course, because the Bible is silent on the matter. But I wonder if, in granting people these visions, Father wants to give hope to multitudes who have suffered the loss of their treasured children, or who are living in deep regret regarding an abortion they had. It does not make abortion right; rather it shows that our God can redeem the most grievous mistakes and turn them to good.

Where is Heaven?

Most people have a concept that heaven is up and hell is down. This stems from the Bible's use of these terms. For example, Jesus warns the city of Capernaum that God will cast

---

8 There is no age of accountability or innocence identified as such in Scripture. The Lord in his wisdom did not identify a specific moment. God alone knows when each soul is accountable, when real rejection has taken place, when the love of sin exists in the heart and when enmity with God is conscious and wilful. What then happens to children who die before this age of accountability? Do they go to heaven? The answer is 'yes,' and it is a strong 'YES,' based upon the confidence of King David who, when his little baby died, said, "He cannot come to me, but I shall go to him." And David knew he was going to paradise (see 2 Samuel 12:21-23). It would appear then that God treats children prior to the age of accountability as innocent. It does not mean that they are not fallen or that they are not sinful; rather it means that God mercifully treats them as innocent in spite of that, and exercises grace to do that, just as he exercises grace to save those who believe. (Adapted from www.gty.org/resources/articles/A264/the-age-of-accountability, accessed 5/1/16).

it down to hell on Judgment Day.[9] When Jesus returned to heaven after his death and resurrection, the Bible says that he *ascended* into heaven. The scriptures record, "He was taken up before their very eyes, and a cloud hid him from their sight. They were looking intently up into the sky as he was going, when suddenly two men dressed in white stood beside them. 'Men of Galilee,' they said, 'why do you stand here looking into the sky? This same Jesus, who has been taken from you into heaven, will come back in the same way you have seen him go into heaven.'"[10]

The apostle Paul says he was *caught up* to heaven.[11] Similarly, John saw an open door into heaven and the Lord told him to *come up* here.[12] Hell may well be in the bowels of the earth, and heaven may well be beyond the stars of space. Unfortunately, this fosters a belief, as referred to in chapter three, that heaven is very far way and inaccessible, except by death. This stems from the ancient Greek thinking that influenced the church of antiquity. The Greek gods were thought of as spending most of their time far away from earth in a type of cosmic equivalent of Hawaii. But our God is not far off; he is always near us.

The use of the terms up and down may be God's timeless way to help people of all ages understand heaven and hell. Science postulates that parallel universes might exist. Whether this is true or not is unknown, but perhaps heaven is not so much up, but near – all around us but in another realm. Perhaps a vision of heaven is merely stepping through one realm into another.

---

9 Luke 10:15
10 Acts 1:9-11 (NIV)
11 2 Corinthians 12:2
12 Revelation 4:1

The Lord has left the location of heaven a mystery. The simple 'up' satisfies most, while others may use the word 'around'. The major point the Bible makes is that wherever heaven and hell may be, we are to seek to reach heaven and to avoid hell.

Activity in Heaven

What do people do in heaven? Again, gleaning from the Bible, and both historic and contemporary visions, we may conclude that heaven is a very active place. For a start, holy angels and perfected believers have the enormous privilege of seeing God face-to-face and worshipping before his throne.[13] Worship there is far beyond anything we experience on earth. To see the Father and Jesus in their fullness must elicit the most heartfelt and vibrant worship and praise. No doubt, music in heaven will also be more beautiful than the very best earth can produce.

However, heaven is not only about worship. It is also about relationship and service. The city of God is a bustling place with people coming and going, chatting with one another, meeting in each other's mansions, sharing their stories, exploring the beauty of heaven's gardens, learning earth history from God's perspective, and discovering God's glorious eternal plans for the future. I don't believe that the saints in heaven become all-knowing on reaching that realm, but they will have a far more advanced ability to learn and understand.

The greatest privilege, of course, is spending time with Jesus – walking and talking with him. It appears that he and the Father are accessible to all. Heaven is like a multi-faceted jewel

13 See Revelation 7:9-11

– one vision will describe only a tiny aspect of its inexhaustible features. At the heart of it all is the fact that heaven is a place of perfected love. Relationships are inclusive and not exclusive as they often are on earth. No one feels left out. Everyone feels loved and valued. All are honoured. This is what Jesus purchased for us on the cross. Heaven is a family, the family of God.

Father's Family

"For this reason I kneel before the Father," writes the apostle Paul, "from whom every family in heaven and on earth derives its name."[14] According to this statement, all human families originate in the Father, and there are families on earth and in heaven. While there is no marriage in heaven, no doubt family links will still be important. However, I believe that there is another layer of meaning hidden in this verse.

The King James Version alludes to it when it says, "… from whom the whole family in heaven and earth is named."

The church is one family, comprising living believers on earth and departed believers in heaven. Thus the living and the dead are not separated in relationship, merely in geography. "If we live, it's to honour the Lord. And if we die, it's to honour the Lord," states the book of Romans. "So whether we live or die, we belong to the Lord. Christ died and rose again for this very purpose – to be Lord of both the living and of the dead."[15] Dead believers form the church in heaven, and living ones form the church on earth; but it is one church, one family. Though

14 Ephesians 3:14-15 (NIV)
15 Romans 14:8-9

the two parts of this family are separated for a time, there will be a wonderful reunion at Christ's return. In fact, the saints in heaven long for this.

"Therefore, since we are surrounded by such a great cloud of witnesses," exhorts the Bible, "let us throw off everything that hinders and the sin that so easily entangles. And let us run with perseverance the race marked out for us."[16]

This cloud of witnesses are the people of faith mentioned in the previous scriptures[17] whose faithful lives are thus a witness or testimony to us. However, some believe that it also means that the believers in heaven are permitted to glimpse or witness our progress on earth, something I agree with.

Like heavenly spectators in the arena of life, departed believers cheer us on in the spiritual race we are running on earth. Witnesses see things. While I do not believe that believers in heaven are all-seeing and know everything about our journey as God does, I do believe that he allows them to glimpse the church's journey on earth[18] and how we are progressing.[19]

---

16 Hebrews 12:1

17 See Hebrews 11

18 For example, the martyrs in Revelation 6:9-11 were aware of events unfolding on earth.

19 This begs the question, "Do believers in heaven feel concern?" If heaven is paradise, surely there would be no sadness or anxiety? Yet scripture says that the Lord grieves or gets angry concerning events on earth and he is in heaven. True blissful joy may not come until the new heaven and earth is created when God will wipe away every tear. So there may be concern as the church in heaven views our race on earth. However they have a huge advantage – they behold the face of God and can see his purposes much more clearly; purposes and plans that will overcome all the enemy's strategies, as long as the church on earth walks dependently on God.

And they spur us on. Not only does the record of their lives shout to us, but one can also imagine their voices resounding with exhortations such as: "Trust in the Lord! Be strong! Be courageous! The Lord loves you! Have faith! Finish the race! Keep your eye on the prize!" Why might they be so interested in our race? Why would they urge us on so strongly? The answer is found in the previous verses: "All these people earned a good reputation because of their faith, yet none of them received all that God had promised. For God had something better in mind for us, so that they would not reach perfection without us."[20]

Longing in Heaven

They cheer us on not only to encourage us, but also because of the deep longing in their hearts. Longing in heaven? Yes. Simply put, they know they can only receive the prize they have been waiting for when the last generation of believers on earth crosses the finish line, and the full harvest of lost souls has been gathered in. What is that prize? It is the return of Christ to the earth, with them; the obtaining of new resurrection bodies, the reuniting of the church on earth, and in heaven, to form a beautiful bride, and the marriage of this bride to Christ, so that together they can reign over a new earth filled with righteousness, glory, and beauty.

"It [grace] teaches us to say 'No' to ungodliness and worldly passions," records the apostle Paul, "and to live self-controlled, upright and godly lives in this present age, while we wait for the blessed hope – the appearing of the glory of our great God and

---

20 Hebrews 11:39-40

Saviour, Jesus Christ."[21] Hope does not cease in heaven. Both heaven and earth long for this blessed hope.

The church in heaven is perhaps more aware of the counsels of God than the church on earth, just as spectators in an arena, due to their elevated position, can see more of the game than the players on the field. This increases their longing for us to run our race well, and reach a lost world both God and they love. They know that when we cross the line, they win too. This should motivate us to live our lives with passion and resolve, serving the Lord and his Kingdom purposes. For example, Greta and I seek to serve the Lord the best we can, conscious that Jane and Ron are in the great cloud of witnesses described above. By living faithful lives, we want to give them something to cheer about, as well as bring pleasure to our Lord. It is as if we have one foot on earth and one foot in heaven.

The saints in heaven also long for the physical realm of earth. "The heavens belong to the LORD," records the psalmist, "but he has given the earth to all humanity."[22] Earth is humankind's home. Heaven is the home of God and his angels and the temporary home of departed believers. But we were meant for earth. As we shall see in a later chapter, God is so committed to this that he will eventually bring his home of heaven upon a newly fashioned earth and live with us forever.

As wonderful as heaven is now, and as delightful as it must be to live in Paradise, God has wisely set a longing in the hearts of those in heaven, for earth. How strange that, while believers on earth long for heaven, believers in heaven long for earth,

---

21 Titus 2:12-13 (NIV)
22 Psalm 115:16

albeit the new one that is to come!

As well, believers in heaven yearn for their resurrection bodies. At present they are perfected spirits. But they look forward to the day when they will be clothed with perfect resurrection bodies suited to living upon the new earth. The apostle Paul makes this clear when he says, "For we will put on heavenly bodies; we will not be spirits without bodies."[23] And we on earth also long for that. In fact, the whole creation groans now, waiting for the full restoration to paradise when Jesus returns. "For we know that all creation has been groaning as in the pains of childbirth right up to the present time," writes Paul. "And we believers also groan … for we long for our bodies to be released from sin and suffering. We, too, wait with eager hope for the day when God will give us our full rights as his adopted children, including the new bodies he has promised us."[24]

There is no groan in heaven, for they have been freed from the pains of earth, but there is longing. And this motivates the believers there to action, especially prayer.

Prayer in Heaven

In heaven, Jesus prays. And, I believe, departed believers do too. "Christ Jesus died for us and was raised to life for us," records the Bible, "and he is sitting in the place of honour at God's right hand, pleading for us."[25] If the head prays, then the body, both on earth and in heaven, prays. I have no doubt that

---

23 2 Corinthians 5:3
24 Romans 8:22-23
25 Romans 8:34

the church in heaven intercedes for the church on earth and for God's Kingdom to invade this world. As the cloud of witnesses to our race, they not only exhort us on, but make petitions to God. A hint of this is seen in the book of Revelation when the martyrs in heaven passionately petition God for justice: "How long, Sovereign Lord, holy and true, until you judge the inhabitants of the earth and avenge our blood?"[26] Now we are not to pray to the saints in heaven asking them to entreat God for us, as some denominations teach. There is only one mediator between God and humanity – Jesus Christ our saviour.[27] They pray for us; we are not to pray to them but to God alone.

If the rich man in Hades pleaded with Abraham to be released from his torment – a prayer that could not be answered – how much more do we suppose that those in heaven are able to pray?

When my first wife Jane passed away, one of our sons came back to the Lord soon after. He knew his mother prayed for him constantly on earth and perhaps figured that, now she was in heaven with direct access to God, his days of straying were numbered! Those in heaven are like Esthers who have literally come into the throne room of God, whose sceptre of acceptance and openness to their requests are extended towards them.[28]

The most effective prayers on earth are those prayed with heavenly perspective, for Jesus told us to pray that God's will would be done on earth as it is in heaven. When we discover what heaven wants, and intercede for that, answers come. Think

---

26 Revelation 6:10 (NIV)

27 See John 16:24. We are to ask the Father in Jesus' name, not anyone else's.

28 See Esther 5:2-3

then of the much clearer view a believer would have in heaven, and the prayers that might spring from that.

One day all intercession will cease, time will end and a new, perfect order will begin. Until then, Christ's body, comprising perfected believers in heaven and still-being-perfected believers on earth, intercede that his kingdom come and his will be done.

Renowned hymn writer and theologian Isaac Watts[29] wrote:

> But is all heaven made up of praises? Is there no prayer there? Does not every separate spirit there, look and long for the resurrection … waiting for the redemption of the body? And may we not suppose each holy soul sends a sacred and fervent wish after this glorious day, and lifts up a desire to its God about it? May it not, under the influence of divine love, breathe out the requests of its heart, and the expressions of its zeal, for the glory and kingdom of Christ? May not the church above join with the churches below, in this language, 'Father, thy kingdom come, thy will be done on earth as it is in heaven'?[30]

Conclusion

So what is heaven like? It is a place of indescribable beauty. It is also a place of perfect love and fellowship with God and

---

29 Isaac Watts, 1674-1748.

30 Excerpt from *The Works of the Rev. Isaac Watts D.D. in Nine Volumes*, published 1812.

one another; of heartfelt praise and worship, of longing for the new world, of learning, of joyful pleasure in the presence of God, and of prayer that his eternal purposes be outworked for his church on earth and for a lost world. Heaven is a place of stimulating activity and we have only begun to glimpse a tiny fraction of what it is like. All eternity will be insufficient to discover the fullness of the paradise that God has prepared for those who love him.

chapter eleven

WHAT ABOUT OUR BODIES?

The hot Middle Eastern sun beat down on the tomb where his corpse lay. Dead for four days, Lazarus' body was now beginning to decompose. To his grieving sisters Martha and Mary, Jesus simply said, "Your brother will rise again."[1] This seemed absurd, given that many Jews believed that a person's spirit remained near the body for three days and then departed, removing all possibility of a resurrection. In Martha's mind, surely Jesus was speaking of the resurrection at the last day? Not so. "I am the resurrection and the life," Jesus continued. "The one who believes in me will live, even though they die; and whoever lives by believing in me will never die."[2] Standing in front of the grave, Jesus commanded Lazarus to come out. Suddenly, Lazarus, still bound in his grave clothes, walked out of the tomb, astonishing the onlookers.

---

1 John 11:23
2 John 11:25-26 (NIV)

Perhaps the greatest sign of Jesus' entire ministry, this resurrection preceded his own and signalled the triumphant victory over death that the cross would accomplish. While he would die again, Lazarus' temporary resurrection pointed to the day when all the dead will rise again and live forever, some in heaven and some sadly in hell.

An angel once spoke to the prophet Daniel about the end of time saying, "Many of those whose bodies lie dead and buried will rise up, some to everlasting life and some to shame and everlasting disgrace."[3] Jesus similarly stated, "The time is coming when all the dead in their graves will hear the voice of God's Son and they will rise again. Those who have done good will rise to experience eternal life, and those who have continued in evil will rise to experience judgment."[4]

There will be a day when all the dead of history – from the creation to the end of time – will hear the voice of the Son of God saying, "RISE!" In a moment of time, their bodies shall be raised from the dead, be reunited with their soul and spirit, and become complete again. Even if the ages have reduced them to dust, or cremation has reduced them to ash, those bodies will live again.

The God who sustains the universe by his mighty power, knows where every atom is and can easily bring them together again to recreate a physical body.

Notice that Jesus states there are two resurrections: a resurrection of the righteous and a resurrection of the unrighteous.

---

3 Daniel 12:2

4 John 5:28-29

The First Resurrection

"But those who die in the LORD will live;" declares the prophet Isaiah, "their bodies will rise again! Those who sleep in the earth will rise up and sing for joy! For your life-giving light will fall like dew on your people in the place of the dead!"[5] When exactly will this utterly joyful event occur? God revealed the timing to the apostle Paul: "For the Lord himself will come down from heaven with a commanding shout, with the voice of the archangel, and with the trumpet call of God. First, the believers who have died will rise from their graves. Then, together with them, we who are still alive, and remain on the earth, will be caught up in the clouds to meet the Lord in the air. Then we will be with the Lord forever."[6]

The great hope of the Christian life is the return of Jesus Christ to rule the earth. At that time believers' bodies will be raised from the dead, changed into glorious new bodies (discussed in more detail in the next chapter) and reunited with their spirits, which have been in heaven. Believers still alive at that time will also undergo transformation and receive a glorified body. In modern times, many believers call this event the rapture.[7] In past ages, the church simply called this the resurrection of the saints.

A number of theories about the timing of Jesus' coming, centre mainly on when this rapture occurs, in relation to the great global trials that will characterise the last days.

---

5 Isaiah 26:19

6 1 Thessalonians 4: 16-17

7 The word rapture comes from the Latin rapere, meaning "to seize" or "to snatch." The Latin Bible uses it for the Greek word that is translated "caught up" in English Bibles today.

Regarding the end of time, Jesus warned, "There will be great distress, unequalled from the beginning of the world until now – and never to be equalled again."[8] This time of distress – known as the tribulation – will see a maturity of evil and rebellion that will usher in terrifying events on earth.

Concerning this tribulation, there are various views amongst Christians. Some see it as already having been fulfilled in the first century AD, especially with Nero's vicious persecution of Christians and the destruction of Jerusalem in 70 AD by the Roman army. This is the full *preterist* view (taking place beforehand). Others see the tribulation as taking place all through history – past, present, and future. This is the *historicist* view. Still others believe that it awaits a time in the future and will be seven years in duration. This is the *futurist* view. See the appendix at the end of this chapter for a further explanation of these terms.

Jesus continued, "Immediately after the anguish of those days [the tribulation] … the sign that the Son of Man is coming will appear in the heavens, and there will be deep mourning among all the peoples of the earth. And they will see the Son of Man coming on the clouds of heaven with power and great glory. And he will send out his angels with the mighty blast of a trumpet, and they will gather his chosen ones from all over the world – from the farthest ends of the earth and heaven."[9] This highly visible and powerful return of Christ to earth is called the second coming – Jesus' first coming being his birth as the Saviour.

---

8 Matthew 24:21 (NIV)
9 Matthew 24:29-31

These three events – the tribulation, rapture, and second coming – frame the resurrection of believers' bodies from the dead. Amongst Christians, there are differing views on the timing of these events. Preterists and historicists tend to see the rapture as simultaneous with Christ's second coming, though there are variations of belief within these groups. Among futurists (who have tended to dominate interpretation of end-times events since the early nineteenth century onwards) three main viewpoints occur:

1. Pre-tribulation Rapture:
Jesus snatches the church away before the seven-year tribulation starts, and returns to earth with the church at the end of it. During the tribulation, the church is safe in heaven.

2. Mid-tribulation Rapture:
Jesus snatches the church away in the middle of the tribulation (the last three and a half years of which are the worst, and thus called the Great Tribulation) and returns at the end of it.

3. Post-tribulation Rapture:
Jesus snatches the church away at the end of the tribulation, as he is returning to the earth. In other words, the rapture and the second coming are simultaneous.

Whatever timing proves true in the end, the point to note is that Jesus will return to earth and, when he does, believers will receive glorified, resurrected bodies and will reign with him throughout eternity.

The Second Resurrection

In his startling vision of the end of time, the apostle John records, "Then I saw thrones, and the people sitting on them had been given the authority to judge. And I saw the souls of those who had been beheaded for their testimony about Jesus and for proclaiming the word of God. They had not worshipped the beast or his statue, nor accepted his mark on their foreheads or their hands.

"They all came to life again, and they reigned with Christ for a thousand years. This is the first resurrection. (The rest of the dead did not come back to life until the thousand years had ended.) Blessed and holy are those who share in the first resurrection. The second death has no power, but they will be priests of God and of Christ, and will reign with him a thousand years."[10]

John's vison again emphasises that there will be two resurrections. The first will be the raising of all believers and the second will be the rest of the dead – all those who have not believed in God's Son, and who have rebelled against God. While some believe that the two resurrections will be virtually simultaneous, others believe that a thousand-year period, called the Millennium, will separate the two resurrections.

As with the rapture and second coming, there are also different views about the Millennium:

---

10 Revelation 20:4-6

1. Pre-millennialism:

Christ will return to earth and there will be a literal thousand-year reign by him on earth. Glorified and resurrected believers will rule with him over the nations of humanity that survive the Great Tribulation. Paradise will be restored on earth, all wars will cease and the nations will live in peace and will worship the Lord. During this period, Satan will be bound but then released for a short time at the end of the Millennium. At that time, he will seek to deceive humankind and incite them to rebel against God one last time. The Lord will destroy the rebels and then the final resurrection will occur.

2. Post-millennialism:

An empowered church will, through the proclamation and demonstration of the gospel of the Kingdom, gradually see multitudes saved and global transformation. Together with the outpouring of the Holy Spirit on all humanity, this will establish a golden age on the earth, after which Jesus will return, and then there will be a final resurrection. While some post-millennialists see the thousand years as literal, others see the thousand years more as a figurative term for a long period. Popular in the 18th and 19th centuries, postmillennialism lost favour after World War I, the Great Depression and World War II, as many became disillusioned by the horrors they had witnessed. It is gaining in popularity again today, with the current emphasis on the church being called to bring Kingdom transformation in the earth – a transformation, however, which cannot be completed fully until Christ himself returns, taking over the kingdoms of this world.

3. Amillennialism:

The millennium is not a literal thousand years but is a symbolic number representing perfection and completion. This view holds that the millennium has already begun at Pentecost and is concurrent with the present church age. Christ reigns from heaven and that reign is spiritual not physical. At the end of the church age, Christ will return, the resurrection will occur, the final judgment takes place, and a new heaven and new earth established.

It Will All Work Out in the End

While sincere believers may adhere to any one of these different views, citing scripture to defend their positions, theories about the details of Christ's return should not divide us. I like the man who claimed that he was a *pan-millennialist*. When asked what he meant, he replied, "I believe it will all pan out in the end!" On these three things however, all believers can agree: Jesus will return, there will be resurrection and judgment, and God will restore paradise.

Whatever our views of the thousand-year period, it is clear from John's vision that the second resurrection of non-believers occurs after the resurrection of believers. "There is an order to this resurrection," states the apostle Paul, "Christ was raised as the first of the harvest; then all who belong to Christ will be raised when he comes back."[11] It seems only fitting that God's children are raised before the rest of humankind, who have rejected God.

John goes on to record what happens next: "Then I saw a great white throne and him who was seated on it. The earth and the heavens fled from his presence, and there was no place for them. And I saw the dead, great and small, standing before

---

11 1 Corinthians 15:23

the throne, and books were opened. Another book was opened, which is the book of life.

The dead were judged according to what they had done as recorded in the books. The sea gave up the dead that were in it, and death and Hades gave up the dead that were in them, and each person was judged according to what they had done. Then death and Hades were thrown into the lake of fire. The lake of fire is the second death. Anyone whose name was not found written in the book of life was thrown into the lake of fire."[12]

The predominant view is that the dead mentioned here are the spiritually dead of all history, who have not believed in God and thus not had their sins wiped away. Their spirits are raised from Hades and their bodies are raised out of the grave or the sea. They stand before God in what the Bible calls the Great White Throne judgment. We will explore this judgment in more detail in a later chapter, but for now, it is clear that if anyone's name is not found in the Book of Life, God will throw that person into the lake of fire. Jesus equated this lake of fire with the name Gehenna.[13] For example, he warns, "If your hand causes you to sin, cut it off. It's better to enter eternal life with only one hand than to go into the unquenchable fires of hell [Gehenna in Greek] with two hands."[14]

---

12 Revelation 20:11-15 (NIV)

13 English "Gehenna" represents the Greek Ge'enna, equivalent to the Hebrew Ge Hinnom, literally "Valley of Hinnom". This was a place outside Jerusalem where rubbish was burned, and in older times children sacrificed. Later the Romans used it for cremation. It is thus a fitting term for the lake of fire.

14 Mark 9:43

Two Hells

Confusingly, many English Bibles simply translate the word Gehenna as hell, doing the same for the word Hades. In reality, Hades (temporary hell) and Gehenna (final hell) are two distinct places. Hades is like the remand prison, where the departed souls of the unrighteous (judged individually at death) await public judgment and sentencing. Gehenna is like the state prison, where one is finally sent when sentence is passed. As we shall see later, God's justice demands this final, public trial and sentencing.

God created Gehenna for the devil and his angels. Satan (or Lucifer as he was called) was once one of the most powerful angels in heaven, but rebelled, one third of the angels siding with him. A popular misconception is that the devil, fallen angels, and demons are in hell now, from where they torment humankind. In reality, they are at loose in the world, but know that God will sentence them to hell at the end of time, a thing they greatly fear.[15] Satan is the prince of the power of the air[16] and realises that the Lord will one day cast him into Gehenna. His evil goal is to drag as many people there with him. By deception, he blinds the minds of multitudes so that they cannot understand the gospel that could save them. This is tragic and it is why the church must preach the good news of Christ. It is also why we must pray unceasingly for our unsaved family members,

---

15 See Revelation 20:10 and Matthew 8:29 which state that the devil will be thrown into the lake of fire prior to the second resurrection, along with the demons and fallen angels. (Some fallen angels are already locked in dungeons of gloom, known as Tartarus, awaiting judgment. Apparently God decided to confine some of the fallen angels while allowing others to be free. See 2 Peter 2:4)

16 Ephesians 2:2 (KJV)

neighbours, and others, interceding that harvest will come to the nations and that people will give their lives to Christ.

Because he takes no pleasure in sending people to Gehenna, God sent Jesus, who, through the cross, took the punishment of sin on himself so that he could spare everyone from the terrifying fate of hell. That is outstanding love. "For God did not send his Son into the world to condemn the world," explained Jesus, "but to save the world through him. Whoever believes in him is not condemned, but whoever does not believe stands condemned already because they have not believed in the name of God's one and only Son."[17] For believers, the great hope we have in Christ can be best voiced by Job: "But as for me, I know that my Redeemer lives, and he will stand upon the earth at last. And after my body has decayed, yet in my body I will see God! I will see him for myself. Yes, I will see him with my own eyes. I am overwhelmed at the thought!"[18]

In the next chapter, we will investigate what the Bible says about the remarkable bodies believers will have in the resurrection.

---

17 John 3:17-18(NIV)
18 Job 19:25-27

Appendix

Rather than focus on a timetable for end-time events, the chief purpose of this chapter is to give hope that there is a resurrection from the dead. There are numerous books dealing with the former matters in more detail but, because this can be a confusing topic, here is a brief summary of the three major views[19] of end-time events:

1. Preterism

Preterism (meaning 'gone by') sees prophecy about the end times as being fulfilled mainly in the past, particularly (in the case of the Book of Revelation) during the first century AD. Prophecies in general, therefore, have already been fulfilled, especially during the destruction of Jerusalem in the year 70 AD. There are two major views within preterism: partial preterism (many, but not all, of the end-time prophecies were fulfilled during the lifetime of Jesus and the Early Church) and full preterism (all of the Bible's prophecies were fulfilled during the lifetime of Jesus and the Early Church). Preterist beliefs usually have a close connection to amillennialism.

2. Historicism

Historicism sees end-time prophecy as being fulfilled all through history - past, present and future. In the case of the Book of Revelation, this includes the last two millennia.

---

19 Sourced and edited from http://en.wikipedia.org/wiki/Christian_eschatology, accessed 9/5/2015.

Historicists cite past historical events as examples of prophecies being fulfilled, but with an understanding that prophecy may involve both a near and far fulfilment. That is, it can have both a past and future realisation. As an illustration, take Alpha Centauri, the nearest star to earth apart from the sun. To the naked eye it appears as one star, but a telescope shows it to be a binary star (two stars revolving around a common centre of gravity). Prophecy can be like this – appearing to have a past fulfilment when, in fact, it may also have a future one that becomes apparent the closer we get to the event.

3. Futurism

In futurism, associations may be made with historical events, but most prophecies chiefly refer to events that have not yet been fulfilled, but which will take place at the end of the age. These prophecies will be fulfilled during a global time of chaos known as the Great Tribulation, and afterwards. Futurist beliefs usually have a close association with premillennialism, as popularised by the *Left Behind* series of books and movies.

In my early Christian years, I was a confirmed futurist. In later years, I have come to respect other views, and believe that a combination of elements of all three views is most likely correct. I believe that prophecies concerning end-time events have seen fulfilment in the past, including the first century, yet consider that many most likely have a full and final fulfilment still to come. Time will tell.

We should follow the *this is that* principle. Numerous Old Testament prophecies about Christ's first coming were not understood before they happened. However, the New Testament frequently uses the phrase *this took place to fulfil what was spoken through the prophet* or similar, in describing them being fulfilled at the time. So it will be in the future. As events occur, we will be able to relate them to the prophecies about Christ's second coming and say, "This is that which prophecy predicted." Until then, Christians should focus not on the details surrounding Christ's coming, but on the glorious hope that he is coming back and the dead will be raised to life again. Then we will be with him forever.

chapter twelve

THE BODY YOU WILL HAVE IN THE RESURRECTION

A man once had a vision. He beheld Jesus who introduced him to a tall, stately young man wearing a pure white robe with a gold sash across his chest. A silver band with a gleaming red ruby fixed to the front circled his head. Slim and well built, the young man exuded confidence and authority, tempered with a gentleness and kindness. Though noble and princely, this tall stranger smiled welcomingly and somehow looked strangely familiar. Seeing the man's perplexity, Jesus revealed who this other person was – he was showing him his future glorified, resurrected self. In the eternal dimension in which God dwells, the Lord had allowed present and future to meet. The heavenly man patted his shorter earthly self on the head, saying, "Hello little brother!" This was an incredibly encouraging foretaste of what he would become.

Fiction? Maybe not. To God, past, present, and future is now. He created time for humanity, and is outside of it. Time is God's servant, not his master. Anything is possible for him. While the Bible should be the sole source of sound theological belief and doctrine, visions can at least encourage us to dream. Can you glimpse yourself in that resurrected state? Take a good look: no wrinkles or flaws, no thin or fat, no weakness or sickness, just perfected beauty and strength. Ageless vitality clothed with the radiance of God's glory, and a mind functioning at full capacity, as Adam and Eve had enjoyed in the Garden of Eden (or perhaps even beyond theirs).

You will most probably be taller than you are now, for there is evidence in the fossil record to suggest that the plants, animals, and humans of God's original creation were bigger than they are today, as the stunting caused by genetic deterioration had not yet taken effect. It is likely that God will restore our resurrection bodies to that first design. While it is interesting to speculate, we must actually turn to the Bible for definitive information about the resurrection body. What does it have to say?

"For we know," declares the apostle Paul, "that when this earthly tent we live in is taken down (that is, when we die and leave this earthly body), we will have a house in heaven, an eternal body made for us by God himself and not by human hands … for we will put on heavenly bodies; we will not be spirits without bodies.[1]

We will not be spirits without bodies. This fact gives great hope to the believers in heaven who, at this time, have only spirit bodies; and to believers on earth who groan in their current,

---

1 2 Corinthians 5:1, 3

fading physical bodies. God has prepared for every child of his a new physical body that Paul describes as a heavenly body, in that it will be as superior to our earthly body as heaven is to earth. As the earthly body clothes the spirit now, so the heavenly body will clothe the spirit after the resurrection. Note that Paul likens our present bodies to a tent, or temporary dwelling, whereas he compares our resurrection bodies to a house, a permanent dwelling.

Your heavenly or resurrection body will be very different to that which you have now. It will be like undergoing an extreme, extreme makeover! Influenced by Greek culture, some of the Corinthians to whom Paul wrote these things were incredulous at the thought of a resurrected physical body, and questioned Paul about this. He responded, "But someone may ask, "How will the dead be raised? What kind of bodies will they have?" What a foolish question!"[2] Ancient Greeks believed that, at death, the spirit passed into the afterlife, and that the body remained behind forever. As they considered the physical body a weak, wretched thing anyway, it was laughable to them to conceive of the body being raised from the grave.

Some of the Corinthians were thus asking sceptically about the kind of bodies they would have if a physical resurrection was possible. After rebuking them gently for their cynicism, Paul went on to explain that, in the afterlife, we would not be spirits without bodies; rather we would be spirits with new bodies. Believers in Christ will have bodies suited to live with him forever. The Bible does not describe unbelievers' resurrection bodies, but they will be suited in some way to hell.

---

2 1 Corinthians 15:35-36a

However, it does describe the believer's resurrection body. So what it is it like?

Illustrations of the Resurrection Body

The apostle Paul used three different illustrations in 1 Corinthians 15 to explain what the resurrection body will be like:

1. Botanical

"When you put a seed into the ground," he writes, "it doesn't grow unless it dies first. And what you put into the ground is not the plant that will grow, but only a bare seed of wheat or whatever you are planting. Then God gives it the new body he wants it to have. A different plant grows from each kind of seed."[3]

Someone said, "Christians don't get buried, they get planted!" The resurrection body will be related to the earthly body (the seed) that goes into the grave, but it will be greatly changed. The corn plant, for example, is different to the seed planted, but the genetic identity is the same. The seed 'dies' and becomes a plant that bears fruit. The plant is superior to the seed from which it came.

In the same way, your resurrection body, though recreated and greatly changed, will still be you. Just as the corn seed gives rise to corn and not carrots, so there is an interconnection between your present body and your future body. Though our

---

3 1 Corinthians 15: 36b - 38

bodies will be wonderfully changed, we will still recognise one another.

Males will be raised males; females will be raised females. However, there will be no marriage. "For when the dead rise," explained Jesus, "they will neither marry nor be given in marriage. In this respect they will be like the angels in heaven."[4] Jesus did not say that we would be angels; rather he said we would be like angels. Angels do not marry. There is only one marriage in eternity and that is the church, the Bride of Christ, to Jesus. Relationships in the resurrection will be on a level greater than anything known in this present age. Family will still be special, but in a different sense than to today. This is a relief to Greta and me. When we finally get to meet Ron and Jane again, there will not be the confusion of who is married to whom! The four of us will be like brothers and sisters who will have deep bonds for eternity. We will be part of a huge family of believers, living in perfect love and relationship, with our attention centred on Jesus our Saviour.

2. Zoological

"Similarly there are different kinds of flesh – one kind for humans, another for animals, another for birds, and another for fish."[5]

There are different kinds of bodies for different kinds of living: a fish's body is designed for swimming, whereas a bird's body is designed for flying. An animal's body is adapted for living on

[4] Matthew 22:30
[5] 1 Corinthians 15:39

land, while the human body is adapted for living on land and ruling over creation. As there are different bodies suited to different environments, so the resurrection body will be suited to a new dimension.

At the end of time, God will create a new heaven and earth and the people who live in that realm will not die, get sick, or have any pain or sorrow. They will have bodies suited perfectly to that new sphere.

3. Celestial

"There are also heavenly bodies and there are earthly bodies; but the splendour of the heavenly bodies is one kind, and the splendour of the earthly bodies is another. The sun has one kind of splendour, the moon another and the stars another; and star differs from star in splendour."[6] The beauty of God's creation, even in a fallen state, is spectacular. Who has not been captivated, even enraptured by, a beautiful lake, a wooded forest, or a majestic mountain rising gracefully towards the sky? However, while earthly bodies such as seas, rivers, lakes, forests and mountains are glorious, heavenly bodies such as stars, planets, comets, and galaxies are even more magnificent.

Similarly, just as the glory of celestial systems is far greater than the glory of terrestrial systems, so the body you will have in the resurrection will be far more glorious than the one you have now. In addition, heavenly bodies differ in splendour. This hints that there will be different orders of glory in the resurrection.

---

6 1 Corinthians 15:40-41 (NIV)

"Multitudes who sleep in the dust of the earth will awake," writes the prophet Daniel, "some to everlasting life [believers], others to shame and everlasting contempt [non-believers]. Those who are wise will shine like the brightness of the heavens and those who lead many to righteousness, like the stars forever and ever."[7] Stars shine with differing degrees of radiance. There are small stars and large stars, faint stars and bright stars. There are varying levels of grandeur in the universe. It will be like this when we rise from the dead. Different levels of reward will reflect our service for God and the way we have lived. For example, the twelve apostles will sit on twelve thrones around the throne of God.[8] They will have a great reward in eternity. We will discuss rewards in more detail in the next chapter.

Some might feel demoralised by such a thought and ask, "What hope is there for me?" Jesus taught that the first will be last and the last will be first. Many who have served God faithfully with no visibility on earth, unknown except to heaven, will be highly visible in eternity. Furthermore, in the coming realm of perfect love, there will no jealousy. Instead, there will be great rejoicing at each other's rewards. And while there may be different levels of glory in eternity, all believers' resurrection bodies will have certain things in common.

---

7 Daniel 12:2-3 (NIV)
8 See Matthew 19:28

Characteristics of the Resurrection Body

All resurrection bodies will have the following characteristics in common. They will be:

1. Imperishable

"So will it be with the resurrection of the dead. The body that is sown is perishable, it is raised imperishable."[9] Your resurrection body will be immortal and indestructible. While your present body is subject to sickness, aging, and death, your resurrection body will live forever, free of all those things. There will be no crippled, deformed, sick, underweight or overweight bodies in the resurrection. If you die with one leg, you will be raised with two. If you die blind, you will be raised seeing. God has a plan to restore everything to the way it was when he created the earth. In fact, it will be far better. People may ask what age we will be when we are raised from the dead? Age is actually not a factor in eternity because we will live forever. My belief is that we will be like Adam and Eve when God created them. They were fully mature adults in the prime of their lives.

2. Glorious

"Our bodies are buried in brokenness, but they will be raised in glory."[10] Due to the curse of death and decay inherited from Adam and Eve's fall into sin, our current bodies disappoint us. There is fading strength and memory. Youth is fleeting.

---

9 1 Corinthians 15:42 (NIV)

10 1 Corinthians 15:43a

No matter how great men or women become, they eventually succumb to the limitations of their weakening bodies.

God never designed us to die. He created us to live forever but, because of sin, death came into the world. In almost every human being, there is an inbuilt resistance to aging and death. It is as if we are programmed with a memory of Eden before the fall. We are waiting for the day when God will give us eternal life again.

"We grow weary in our present bodies, and we long to put on our heavenly bodies like new clothing. While we live in these earthly bodies, we groan and sigh, but it's not that we want to die and get rid of these bodies that clothe us. Rather, we want to put on our new bodies so that these dying bodies will be swallowed up by life."[11] We groan now, but we do not moan, because of the hope of what is to come. Our current bodies disappoint us but the resurrection body will be glorious and no longer subject to death, decay, aging or any weakness.

While much of the storyline in the movie *Noah*[12] was distinctly unbiblical, I believe the scriptwriters portrayed one thing correctly: the film depicted Adam and Eve as clothed from head to foot with a glowing light, a manifestation of God's glory. This may explain how, when they sinned, they instantly knew they were naked, as that glory lifted from them. It is likely that God will restore that aura of glory to our resurrected bodies. Jesus, speaking of the resurrection, said, "The righteous will shine like the sun in their Father's Kingdom."[13]

---

11 2 Corinthians 5:2, 4

12 *Noah*, ©2014 Paramount Pictures

13 Matthew 13:43a

3. Powerful

"They are buried in weakness, but they will be raised in strength."[14] Your resurrection body will be like Christ's when he rose from the dead. "For, as in Adam, all die," wrote Paul, "so in Christ all will be made alive. But each in turn: Christ, the firstfruits; then, when he comes, those who belong to him."[15] While the Bible records others as rising from the dead before Jesus did, they all subsequently died again. Jesus arose from death never to die again. In that sense, he is the first fruits, the first of a great harvest of all who have died. "He will take our weak mortal bodies," states the Bible, "and change them into glorious bodies like his own …"[16] This implies that our resurrection bodies will have characteristics similar to his, and be able to do things our current bodies cannot.

Jesus did extraordinary things in his post-resurrection body. For example, he could walk through walls. One time, the disciples were shut in a locked room and Jesus came and stood in their midst. Another time, he disappeared from their sight.[17] Might it be that our resurrection bodies will be able to travel at the speed of thought? Wherever you want to be, you will be there.

Our new bodies will be amazing, beyond what we can possibly imagine. They will not grow old, nor will they ever get tired. They will be powerful and suited completely to living in the new earth and heaven that God will create.

---

14 1 Corinthians 15:43b
15 1 Corinthians 15:22-23 (NIV)
16 Philippians 3:21a
17 See Luke 24:31, John 20:19

4. Spiritual

"They are buried as natural human bodies, but they will be raised as spiritual bodies. For just as there are natural bodies, there are also spiritual bodies."[18] Paul is not meaning that we will be spirits only. He has already stated that we will not be spirits without bodies, as believers in heaven are at present. Rather, he is alluding to the fact that the regenerated spirits of believers are trapped currently in bodies that wage war against the desires of the spirit. The Christian journey is one of progressively allowing our spirits to rule our bodies so that we walk in holiness and purity. Your resurrection body will not have that battle.

The resurrection body will be a spiritual body in that the body and soul will be completely ruled over by the spirit, and subject to God. It will be perfect and incapable of sin. Today, we term a person 'spiritual' if they are zealous in their love, devotion, and obedience to God. This is the sense in which Paul uses the term. As already stated, we will have bodies like Jesus. Was he sinless? Yes. And he will give us sinless bodies like his. That is why in the resurrection there will never be another fall or act of rebellion that will cause Paradise to be lost again.

This spiritual resurrection body will also allow us to see fully into the spiritual realm as well as the physical realm. Now we see the spiritual realm dimly, then we shall see it fully. We will throw off the limitations of our earthly bodies and embrace the freedom of our heavenly bodies. "Earthly people are like the earthly man, and heavenly people are like the heavenly man. Just as we are now like the earthly man, we will someday

---

[18] 1 Corinthians 15:44

be like the heavenly man."[19] Even believers alive at Christ's return will receive a resurrection body: "But let me reveal to you a wonderful secret. We will not all die, but we will all be transformed! It will happen in a moment, in the blink of an eye, when the last trumpet is blown. For when the trumpet sounds, those who have died will be raised to live forever. And we who are living will also be transformed. For our dying bodies must be transformed into bodies that will never die; our mortal bodies must be transformed into immortal bodies."[20]

Our Great Hope

Paul continues, "Then, when our dying bodies have been transformed into bodies that will never die, this Scripture will be fulfilled: 'Death is swallowed up in victory. O death, where is your victory? O death, where is your sting?'"[21] Death has no sting because of the great hope of the resurrection. We need not dread the day of our passing. Death – a glorious doorway to heaven and the resurrection – will allow us to enter the magnificent eternity that God has prepared for those who love him. The apostle John writes, "Dear friends, we are already God's children, but he has not yet shown us what we will be like when Christ appears. But we do know that we will be like him, for we will see him as he really is. And all who have this eager expectation will keep themselves pure, just as he is pure."[22]

---

19 1 Corinthians 15: 48-49
20 1 Corinthians 15: 51-53
21 1 Corinthians 15:54-55
22 1 John 3:2-3

These are some of the greatest words in the Bible: "When he appears we shall be like him." All who have this hope purify themselves. While enjoying all that God provides in this earthly existence, let us not be distracted by the pleasures of life, or be crushed by the suffering common to this planet. Like our present bodies, this earth will not be the way it is forever; something far more wonderful lies ahead. One day we will put off these weak, perishable bodies and put on our glorious resurrection bodies – designed, like new suits of clothing, to live in the magnificent new earth God will create. And there we will live with Jesus forever. "But our citizenship is in heaven," declares the apostle Paul. "And we eagerly await a Saviour from there – the Lord Jesus Christ who, by the power that enables him to bring everything under his control, will transform our lowly bodies, so that they will be like his glorious body."[23]

That is our great hope!

---

[23] Philippians 3: 20-21 (NIV)

chapter thirteen

JUDGMENT DAY

There are books in heaven, and God is their author. In asking God to spare a rebellious Israel from punishment, Moses pleaded, "But now, please forgive their sin – but if not, then blot me out of the book you have written. The LORD replied to Moses, 'Whoever has sinned against me I will blot out of my book.'"[1] This book is called the Book of Life. King David, dismayed by his enemies, wrote, "Erase their names from the Book of Life; don't let them be counted among the righteous."[2]

After a successful ministry trip during which they had seen many healed and delivered from demonic oppression, Jesus' disciples were told, "Do not rejoice that the spirits submit to you, but rejoice that your names are written in heaven."[3] In his letter to the Philippian church, the apostle Paul tells us precisely where in heaven these names are written: "They worked along

---

1 Exodus 32:32-33 (NIV)
2 Psalm 69:28
3 Luke 10:20 (NIV)

with Clement and the rest of my co-workers, whose names are written in the Book of Life."[4]

The Book of Life records the names of all those who have believed in Jesus Christ as their Saviour and Lord.

There is a second type of book in heaven as well. Though not given a specific name in the Bible, it is clearly mentioned. "You saw me before I was born," writes David, "Every day of my life was recorded in your book. Every moment was laid out before a single day had passed."[5] This seems to be some kind of record book in which the details of our entire lives are chronicled. In fact, God writes these details before we are even born. However, the final record of our lives will be shaped by not only what God intended, but also what we actually did. God records all of our thoughts, actions and words in this book. Even our pains and sorrows. David again writes, "You keep track of all my sorrows. You have collected all my tears in your bottle. You have recorded each one in your book."[6] How comforting that every painful thing we endure, and our response to it, is recorded in heaven.

There is a record book for every person, and God will use these books, as well as the Book of Life, on Judgment Day, to determine either reward or punishment. Every human being will have to face a judgment at the end of time. God's justice and love demands this. In his justice, he will punish sin and wrongdoing, and in his love, he will reward faithfulness.

---

4 Philippians 4:3
5 Psalm 139:16
6 Psalm 56:8

The book of Jude contains the earliest recorded prophecy in the Bible and quotes Enoch, a seventh generation descendant of Adam and Eve. "See," declares Enoch, "the Lord is coming with thousands upon thousands of his holy ones to judge everyone, and to convict all of them of all the ungodly acts they have committed in their ungodliness, and of all the defiant words ungodly sinners have spoken against him."[7] In a vision of that coming day, the apostle John wrote, "I saw the dead, both great and small, standing before God's throne. And the books were opened, including the Book of Life. And the dead were judged according to what they had done, as recorded in the books … And anyone whose name was not found recorded in the Book of Life was thrown into the lake of fire."[8]

The prophet Daniel, glimpsing the same judgment day some six hundred years before John, recorded, "I watched as thrones were put in place and the Ancient One sat down to judge … Millions of angels ministered to him; many millions stood to attend him. Then the court began its session, and the books were opened."[9] As Daniel mentions books in plural, it is clear that both the record books and the Book of Life will be used on the Day of Judgment to determine people's destiny.

As we shall see in the next chapter, there are differing views as to the timing of the judgment of believers and non-believers. Some see the judgment of believers as occurring after the rapture and before the resurrection, with the judgment of nonbelievers occurring a thousand years later (premillennial view). Others see the two judgments as simultaneous events occurring at a general

---

7 Jude 14-15 (NIV)
8 Revelation 20:12, 15
9 Daniel 7:9-10

resurrection of all people at the end of the age (amillennial and some postmillennial views). The main point is that there will be a very different outcome for believers and non-believers.

The Judgment of Believers

Writing to believers, the apostle Paul states, "Remember, we will all stand before the judgment seat of God … yes, each of us will give a personal account to God."[10] Imagine standing before Father and Jesus, with all the angels and saints looking on, and having our lives evaluated. On earth, we judge ourselves with bias and tend to excuse wrongdoing in our lives, while seeing it in others; or we condemn ourselves unnecessarily. Not so when we stand before God. His assessment of our lives will be objective and accurate. God will judge (in the sense of evaluate) three things.

Firstly, he will judge our words. "And I tell you this," warned Jesus, "you must give an account on Judgment Day for every idle word you speak. The words you say will either acquit you or condemn you."[11] Secondly, he will evaluate our works. "God will judge us for everything we do," writes wise King Solomon, "including every secret thing, whether good or bad."[12] Thirdly, he will judge our secrets and motives. "Therefore judge nothing before the appointed time," counsels the apostle Paul, "wait until the Lord comes. He will bring to light what is hidden in darkness and will expose the motives of the heart. At that time

---

10 Romans 14:10b, 12.

11 Matthew12:36, 37

12 Ecclesiastes 12:14

each will receive their praise from God."[13]

The thought of their dark secrets being exposed could make some fearful. However, note the phrase 'each will receive their praise from God.' As we shall see later in the chapter, this judgment is to determine our level of reward in eternity, and is not about punishment. Dark secrets can also mean the good things we have done that no-one knows about except God. Not dark in the sense of evil, but in the sense we have kept them in the dark and not told anyone. "Remember," explains the apostle Paul, "the sins of some people are obvious, leading them to certain judgment. But there are others whose sins will not be revealed until later. In the same way, the good deeds of some people are obvious. And the good deeds done in secret will someday come to light."[14] Jesus promised that his Father would openly reward the good things we did in secret.[15] In fact, the Lord desires it to be a time of great joy for all those who have believed in him. Before we look further at this judgment of believers, we need to first clarify what the Lord will not judge.

He Will Not Judge Sin or Salvation

"He who hears my word and believes him who sent me," promised Jesus, "has eternal life; he does not come into judgment but has passed from death to life."[16] Judgment Day will not decide our salvation; we decide that now. Though believers will face a judgment to evaluate their lives, it will not

13 1 Corinthians 4:5 (NIV)
14 1 Timothy 5:24-25
15 See Matthew 6:4,6,18
16 John 5:24 (RSV)

be to determine whether they are saved and eligible for heaven. The apostle John wrote, "I have written this to you who believe in the name of the Son of God, so that you may know you have eternal life."[17]

I grew up in a traditional church, which taught that if you did enough good, attended church, and kept God's commandments, he might let you into heaven. I never knew if I would go to heaven or hell when I died, until somebody said, "You can know. Jesus died for you and you can know now by giving your life to Christ and believing in him." That was a revelation.

God's record books list everything we have done, both good and bad. Because God is so holy and cannot tolerate the slightest sin, one evil thing is enough to condemn us, and exclude our names from the Book of Life. If our name is not in that book, he will sentence us to hell on Judgment Day. As every person on earth has done, said, or thought wrong things, being spared that fate appears to be hopeless. This is bad news, really bad news. However, there has to be bad news before there can be good news. If we treat sin lightly, we will treat the concept of a Saviour lightly.

Sin is a debt. It is like a mortgage on our lives. The word 'mortgage' is an old French legal term meaning 'death pledge or death contract'. The pledge or contract ends (dies) when either the debt is repaid or the property is taken through foreclosure. However, our sin is so great that it cannot be repaid. "Redemption does not come so easily," states the psalmist, for no one can ever pay enough to live forever and never see

---

17 1 John 5:13

the grave."[18] Hence, foreclosure is certain. The foreclosure on our house (body) is death. "For the wages of sin is death," records the Bible.[19] But the debt doesn't end there. In older times, debtors who could not repay their loans were thrown into debtor's prison.[20] The debtor's prison for sin is hell, from which there is no escape. Just as a bank records every last cent of someone's debt, so the books in heaven record every detail of the things we have done, and this record condemns us.

However there is wonderful news: "You were dead because of your sins and because your sinful nature was not yet cut away. Then God made you alive with Christ, for he forgave all our sins. He *cancelled the record of the charges against us* and took it away by nailing it to the cross."[21] When we turn from our wrongdoing and turn to Christ, God rips the mortgage of sin up. All the wrong things we have ever done, said, or thought, are blotted out of the record books. Only the good things remain. And our names are written in the Book of Life. We cannot earn this; it is a gift from a loving God and Saviour. Jesus suffered punishment in our place when he was nailed to the cross. The cross was the judgment for our sin, and what was judged there will not be judged again. Not only has the Father cleared our debt, but he has also taken Jesus' perfect record of righteousness and deposited it into our account. "The free gift of God is eternal life through Christ Jesus our Lord," announces the Bible.[22] No wonder this is called the gospel or good news. It is very, very good news. As King David put it, "What joy for

18 Psalm 49:8-9
19 Romans 6:23a
20 See Matthew 18:30
21 Colossians 2:13-14
22 Romans 6:23b

those whose record the LORD has cleared of guilt."[23]

The late Roland Buck, an American pastor, told of an occasion when he visited heaven in a vision. God showed him the records of all his people and asked if he would like to see one. Buck asked to see Abraham's record and, on reading it, was astonished to see only good things written in it. "Where are the bad things Abraham did?" he asked. God replied, "There is no record of these, as there cannot be two records of the same thing. All the bad things belong to Jesus' record, for he became sin, and it cannot be on Abraham's record at the same time."

Have You Paid?

When Greta and I were in the United Kingdom a few years ago, we visited the picturesque village of Bradford-Upon-Avon in Wiltshire. Entering an award-winning tearoom tracing its origins back to Victorian times, we enjoyed tea and cheesecake, while soaking up the atmosphere of the centuries-old building. Upon finishing, we thanked the staff enthusiastically, and left. Pausing to take a photograph of Greta in front of the building, I was interrupted by the owner who demanded rather sternly, "Have you paid?"

I had been so caught up in the delight of the experience that I had forgotten to pay! Returning inside rather sheepishly, I paid the bill, and apologised for my absent-mindedness. "Have you paid?" will be a question God will ask every person when we stand before him. For those who have believed in Jesus Christ and yielded their lives to him, they will answer, "Jesus has paid for me."

---

[23] Psalm 32:2

People today claim that there are many paths to God. From what we have shown, it is clear that there is only one way.

No religious leader in history, apart from Christ, gave his life for the sin of the world. They all lie dead in their graves, but Jesus arose and lives. Jesus himself said, "I am the way, the truth, and the life. No one can come to the Father except through me."[24]

God says, "I will never again remember their sins and lawless deeds."[25] Consequently, the judgment of Christians is not a judgment of our salvation or sin; instead, it is an evaluation of our service to God since becoming believers, to determine our level of reward in eternity. It will be like a great prize-giving ceremony. "I am coming soon," assures Jesus. "My reward is with me, and I will give to each person according to what they have done."[26] Notice that reward, not punishment, is with him for the believer. "For God is not unjust," says the Bible. "He will not forget how hard you have worked for him and how you have shown your love to him by caring for other believers, as you still do."[27]

How Will Christ Judge Our Lives?

When writing to the believers at Corinth, the apostle Paul states, "For we must all stand before Christ to be judged. We will each receive whatever we deserve for the good or evil we have done in this earthly body."[28] The word 'evil' in the original language of the New Testament is the Greek word *kakos*. It

---

24 John 14:6
25 Hebrews 10:17
26 Revelation 22:12 (NIV)
27 Hebrews 6:10
28 2 Corinthians 5:10

means evil or bad. For example, I could say, "That's a really bad paint job," because it is poor in quality. Now, poor-quality Christian living and service is evil in God's eyes, but as he has forgiven every sin in our lives, *kakos* is better understood here as meaning worthless.

"For it is by grace you have been saved, through faith," explains Paul, "and this is not from yourselves, it is the gift of God – not by works, so that no one can boast. For we are God's handiwork, created in Christ Jesus to do good works, which God prepared in advance for us to do."[29] In other words, our salvation cannot be earned through the things we do, but is entirely gifted to us by a gracious Saviour.

However, once saved, there are works that God has prepared long ago for us to do – assignments, tasks, and commissions. In fact, those works prove that our faith is genuine. Faith, apart from works, according to the Bible, is dead.[30] The Christian life is one of progressively knowing and loving God better, and doing the works he has prepared for us to do.

Given his amazing grace towards us, we should be eager to do these works well. Thus, when Christ judges believers, he will evaluate our works and service since coming to know him, in order to determine if they are good or worthless.

How will Jesus judge our works? The answer is by fire. The apostle Paul explains in detail how this will happen: "Because of God's grace to me, I have laid the foundation like an expert builder. Now others are building on it. But whoever is building

---

29 Ephesians 2:8-10 (NIV)
30 See James 2:14-17

on this foundation must be very careful. For no-one can lay any foundation other than the one we already have – Jesus Christ.

"Anyone who builds on that foundation may use a variety of materials – gold, silver, jewels, wood, hay, or straw. But on the judgment day, fire will reveal what kind of work each builder has done. The fire will show if a person's work has any value. If the work survives, that builder will receive a reward. But if the work is burned up, the builder will suffer great loss. The builder will be saved, but like someone barely escaping through a wall of flames."[31]

Jesus is the foundation of our lives. If he is not the foundation, then anything we build will not endure the fire. God will reward good works of service and growth in character; the bad works he will burn up. This is not a judgment of comparison where we complain, "They received a larger reward than me." This is a judgment of our realised potential, where the Lord says, "This is what I gave you. I gave you my Son, the gift of salvation and relationship with me, and abilities from birth. I gave you my Holy Spirit, spiritual gifts, and my church to nourish you. Now let's see how well you did."

Two Categories of Works

Note that Paul lists two categories of works. The first is gold, silver and jewels, which are non-combustible. The second is wood, hay and straw, all of which are combustible. The fire of God will test everyone's works. Works of gold, silver and jewels will endure the flame and will be refined. Works of wood, hay

31 1 Corinthians 3:10-15

and straw will burn up because they are worthless. We may ask, "What determines whether something is gold, silver and precious stones so that it remains?" The Bible is clear: "And now these three remain: faith, hope and love."[32] What remains? Works of faith, hope, and love. "We remember before our God and Father," writes Paul, "your work produced by faith, your labour prompted by love, and your endurance inspired by hope in our Lord Jesus Christ."[33] Works done in faith, labour done in love, and trials of life endured in hope, will remain at the judgment by fire.

You may say, "What if I have nothing; what if everything gets burned up?" Someone would have to live very carelessly and foolishly to obtain no reward. God will reward even the littlest thing done for him. Jesus said that even a cup of cold water given in his name would not go without its reward.[34] In addition, some of the things we thought were great may go up in smoke, and some of the things we thought were useless may come out as gold. "Oh that was terrible Lord," we say, but he replies, "No that was good. Because you felt weak, my power could work through you." In the celebrity culture prevalent on earth today, people notice stars. Heaven, however, notices servants. Judgment Day will reveal eternity's true heroes. Jesus put it like this: "Many who are the greatest now will be least important then, and those who seem least important now will be the greatest then."[35]

---

32 1 Corinthians 13:13 (NIV)
33 1 Thessalonians 1:3 (NIV)
34 See Matthew 10:42
35 Mark 10:31

A Judgment Story

I once heard the following story about the judgment day of believers. It may not be theologically correct, but it beautifully illustrates the point. Waiting in a great line of people to take his turn before the judgment seat of Christ, a man nervously says to himself, "Oh my, what am I going to say to the Lord? I haven't done all that much with my life and I've got to give an account." As he waits, he decides to talk to the person in front of him. He taps his shoulder and the person turns around. It is the apostle Paul! He thinks, "Oh no, I'm behind the apostle Paul; he's going to get a huge reward and I'm going to get nothing."

To cheer himself up he then turns to the person behind him. To his shock, it is Mother Teresa. "Oh give me a break, this is not fair, I haven't done anything like these two." Then in the distance, he notices his wife and two children standing before the Lord. Jesus talks to them and then says in a loud voice, "Who is the husband and father of this family?" Timidly the man goes forward and stands with his wife and children. Then the Lord says to him, "Well done good and faithful servant. You have loved your wife as I loved the church and you have raised your children in the faith so that they are here today."

It Is All About Faithfulness

Jesus will reward faithfulness in using what he has given us. We do not have to be Mother Teresa or the apostle Paul to obtain a reward. The Father has given differing gifts and abilities to everyone. It is not the size of what we have received or done; it is how faithfully we have used what God has given us, whether small or great. We may have done some worthless things since coming to know the Lord and the fire will burn those things up. It actually will be a great relief that we will not take those things into eternity. What remains – the gold, silver and jewels – will form the basis of our reward.

Many believe they will be fashioned into crowns that we will wear in eternity.[36] Whether these are literal crowns or symbolic is unknown. As crowns represent authority, this indicates that people's rewards may be differing levels of rank and rulership in the new heaven and earth. Eternity will be functional, and purposeful; there will be work, there will be worship, there will be tasks to do and we will rule with Christ. The Bible says we are even going to judge and rule over angels.[37]

It will not only be our service that will be rewarded on that day. God will also reward growth in character, especially the way that we have handled suffering and the trials of life. "For our light and momentary troubles," writes the apostle Paul, "are achieving for us an eternal glory that far outweighs them

---

36 There are six mentions of crowns in the New Testament:
1. An Imperishable Crown – for those who run the race of life well. 1 Corinthians 9:24-27 (NKJV)
2. The Crown of Rejoicing – for soul winners. 1 Thessalonians 2:19-20
3. The Crown of Righteousness – for those who yearn for Christ's return and live accordingly. 2 Timothy 4:7-8
4. The Crown of Life – for those who patiently endure trial and temptation. James 1:12
5. The Crown of Glory – for true leaders who shepherd Christ's church well. 1 Peter 5:2-4 (NIV)
6. The Crown of Gold – for the twenty-four elders, those from the Old and New Testaments, who have attained to the highest reward among God's people. Revelation 4:4
While it is probable that there are six separate crowns, some names may overlap and describe the same crown. For example, an imperishable crown may be a general description of all the crowns and not a separate category.

37 See 1 Corinthians 6:3

all."[38] The book of Revelation, chapters two and three, mentions some of the incredible rewards that Jesus promises to those who overcome sin and adversity.

Everyone who is victorious will:

- Eat from the tree of life in the paradise of God. (2:7)
- Be unhurt by the second death [hell] (2:11)
- Eat from the manna that has been hidden away in heaven and be given a new name. (2:17)
- Be given authority over all the nations." (2: 2)
- Be clothed in white." (3:5)
- Become pillars in the Temple of God and will never have to leave it. (3:12)
- Sit with Christ on his throne." (3:21)

These rewards suggest that, not only will believers live forever and be spared hell, but they will eat heavenly food, be given a new name or identity, be beautifully clothed, never have to leave God's presence, and rule and reign with Christ over his restored creation. These are exceptional rewards for those who overcome.

Now, the extreme worst case is that the fire burns everything up and nothing is left. Paul says that if the work is burned up the builder will suffer great loss. The builder will be saved, but

---

38 2 Corinthians 4:17 (NIV)

like someone barely escaping through a wall of flames. In such a case, there could be a sense of sorrow and regret for a time – perhaps not all of eternity (in the new earth God will wipe away every tear) – but the person will still be saved. They will spend eternity with God, enjoying his presence forever, though perhaps not attaining to the eternal rank they might otherwise have had. However, why just scrape in? We should aim to enter eternity with great reward, for the reward glorifies the Lord. As already stated, we really would have to live very carelessly and foolishly to have nothing.

The Right Attitude

So what should our attitude be? We should not be fearful of judgment; we all make mistakes and they will disappear in the fire. However, we should be sober and motivated to live lives of purity and purpose. If we permit the Holy Spirit to work in our hearts and burn out the wood, hay, and straw now, then it will save us from seeing everything disappear in the fire on judgment day. Whether the good we do is small or great, whether it is just in our neighbourhood or God takes us to the ends of the earth, it does not matter. It is doing the things that God has asked us to do, and doing them well. Though originally written to slaves, the following verse is applicable to all servants of God: "Work willingly at whatever you do, as though you were working for the Lord rather than for people. Remember that the Lord will give you an inheritance as your reward, and that the Master you are serving is Christ."[39]

---

39 Colossians 3:23 & 24

We need to have something at the end of our lives that glorifies Jesus, which makes his dying for us worth it. We want to bring a smile to God's face on Judgment Day, and we want to be able to smile at him. And this is gloriously possible. The Bible says, "Now to him who is able to keep you from falling, and to present you without blemish before the presence of his glory with rejoicing."[40] God will help us. He is able to perfect us and make the day of our judgment a joyful graduation.

I believe that the Father longs for the day when he is able to reward his children. In a recent encounter I had with the Lord, he told me, "I am utterly committed to working in your life, so that you will stand before me with joy. The cross demonstrated this commitment, and having started a good work in you, I will complete it." The Bible promises, "As we live in God, our love grows more perfect. So we will not be afraid on the day of judgment, but we can face him with confidence because we live like Jesus here in this world."[41]

In the next chapter, we will see what happens to non-believers on the Day of Judgment.

---

40 Jude 24 (RSV)

41 1 John 4:17

chapter fourteen

THE JUDGMENT OF THE UNRIGHTEOUS

Justice, according to the dictionary, means *the due allocation of reward of virtue* and *punishment of vice*.[1] If God is just, then there cannot be only a judgment of reward for believers, but there must also be a judgment of punishment for the unrighteous. There is something built into the human heart that longs for justice and cheers when it comes. "A day of anger is coming," warns the apostle Paul, "when God's righteous judgment will be revealed. He will judge everyone according to what they have done. He will give eternal life to those who keep on doing good, seeking after the glory and honour and immortality that God offers. But he will pour out his anger and wrath on those who live for themselves, who refuse to obey the truth and instead live lives of wickedness."[2] Some may escape earthly justice; however, no one will escape God's justice.

---

1 The Concise Oxford Dictionary, Oxford, Oxford University Press, 1982

2 Romans 2:5b-8

More Christians are dying for their faith today than at any other time in history.[3] It seems that everywhere, Christianity is under assault. This apparent triumph of evil can be hard to handle, unless we understand that a day of reckoning is coming. While believers are told to forgive those who persecute them,[4] this does not mean that the perpetrators will escape the consequences of their actions. "In his justice he will pay back those who persecute you," wrote the apostle Paul to the suffering church in Thessalonica, "And God will provide rest for you who are being persecuted and also for us when the Lord Jesus appears from heaven. He will come with his mighty angels, in flaming fire, bringing judgment on those who don't know God, and on those who refuse to obey the Good News of our Lord Jesus. They will be punished with eternal destruction, forever separated from the Lord and from his glorious power."[5]

Separation is Coming

In his teachings, Jesus made it clear that a day of separation is coming. Currently, all humankind cohabits planet earth, but it will not always be this way. In explaining about the Kingdom of God, Jesus taught a number of parables about this future separation. In the parable of the wheat and the weeds, for example, a farmer sowed a field of wheat, but overnight an enemy came and sowed tares or darnel, a weed that closely resembles wheat in its juvenile form. Only when the wheat and tares have formed ears of grain, are the two distinguishable. Grain from darnel is bitter, even toxic, and if mixed with wheat

---

3 Various internet sources quote figures of 100,000-165,000 Christians being martyred each year.

4 See Romans 12:17-19

5 2 Thessalonians 1:6-9

taints it. So it must be separated.

"The field is the world," explained Jesus, "and the good seed represents the people of the Kingdom. The weeds are the people who belong to the evil one. The harvest is the end of the world, and the harvesters are the angels. Just as the weeds are sorted out and burned in the fire, so it will be at the end of the world. The Son of Man will send his angels, and they will remove from his Kingdom everything that causes sin and all who do evil. And the angels will throw them into the fiery furnace, where there will be weeping and gnashing of teeth. Then the righteous will shine like the sun in their Father's Kingdom."[6]

In the parable of the fishing net, Jesus reiterated, "Again, the Kingdom of Heaven is like a fishing net that was thrown into the water and caught fish of every kind. When the net was full, they dragged it up onto the shore, sat down, and sorted the good fish into crates, but threw the bad ones away. That is the way it will be at the end of the world. The angels will come and separate the wicked people from the righteous, throwing the wicked into the fiery furnace, where there will be weeping and gnashing of teeth."[7] This will include not only those alive at the time, but all the dead of history: "The time is coming when all the dead in their graves will hear the voice of God's Son, and they will rise again. Those who have done good will rise to experience eternal life, and those who have continued in evil will rise to experience judgment."[8] God will hold every person accountable for what they have done, especially whether they have accepted or rejected his kind offer of salvation through his son.

---

6 Matthew 13:38-43
7 Matthew 13:47-50
8 John 5:28-29

The Bible warns that, in the last days, nations will rage against the laws of God, rebelling against him; yet multitudes will also come into the Kingdom of God. This is because the wheat and tares will grow to full maturity simultaneously before the Lord returns. God waits, wanting as many to be saved as possible, before the inevitable Day of Judgment dawns.

The apostle John recorded a vision of this future event: "I saw thrones, and the people sitting on them had been given the authority to judge. And I saw the souls of those who had been beheaded for their testimony about Jesus and for proclaiming the word of God … they all came to life again, and they reigned with Christ for a thousand years. This is the first resurrection. (The rest of the dead did not come back to life until the thousand years had ended.)"[9] As explained in chapters eleven and thirteen, Christians differ as to the timing of these events.[10]

---

9 Revelation 20:4-5

10 Some Christians believe that the Bible reveals three separate judgments to come. The first is a judgment of believers' works after the rapture to determine degrees of reward. The second is the judgment of the sheep and goat nations (Matthew 25:31-36). This takes place after the tribulation period but before the millennium. Its purpose is to determine who will enter Christ's millennial kingdom, a literal thousand-year period. The third is the great white throne judgment (see next few pages) at the end of the millennium (Revelation 20:11-15). This is the judgment of unbelievers in which they are judged according to their works and sentenced to everlasting punishment in hell. Other Christians believe that these three judgments speak of the same final event, not of three different judgments. In other words, the great white throne judgment will be the time that believers and unbelievers alike are judged. Those whose names are found in the Book of Life will be judged for their deeds, in order to determine the rewards they will receive. Those whose names are not in the Book of Life will be judged according to their deeds, to determine the degree of punishment they will receive in the lake of fire.

One thing is indisputable however: both the righteous and the unrighteous will face judgment, and there will be two very different outcomes. As detailed in the previous chapter, the judgment of the righteous will be a judgment of reward. The judgment of the unrighteous, however, will be a judgment of punishment.

The Great White Throne Judgment

"And I saw a great white throne and the one sitting on it," records John. "The earth and sky fled from his presence, but they found no place to hide. I saw the dead, both great and small, standing before God's throne. And the books were opened, including the Book of Life. And the dead were judged according to what they had done, as recorded in the books.

The sea gave up its dead, and death and the grave [Hades in Greek] gave up their dead. And all were judged according to their deeds. Then death and the grave were thrown into the lake of fire. This lake of fire is the second death. And anyone whose name was not found recorded in the Book of Life was thrown into the lake of fire."[11]

Here the phrases sea and death giving up their dead refer to a bodily resurrection from the grave. Hades refers to the place of torment where the spirits of the unrighteous are sent upon judgment at death, awaiting this final, public trial and sentencing. Their spirits are reunited with their resurrection bodies and they stand before the throne of the Father. God will open the record books and check everything people have

---

11 Revelation 20:11-15

ever done. He will especially highlight the times they had an opportunity to believe in Christ but rejected him. They had a chance to read his word, listen to the Christian workmate who tried to explain the gospel to them, or heed the family member who was trying to tell them that Jesus could save them. But they would not listen and therefore their record of sin could not be blotted out of the books. No excuses will be offered and every mouth will fall mute before the judge of all the earth, for the books will contain the evidence that will silence them.

Finally, God will check to see if their names are in the Book of Life. I believe there is a space in the Book of Life for every person who has ever lived, for God wants all to be saved. How sad that blanks will be there on judgment day. If their name is not found, then he will cast them into the lake that burns with fire and sulphur, called Gehenna (translated 'hell' in English). Furthermore, the record books will determine their level of punishment in hell.

Levels of Punishment in Hell

Gehenna is a terrible place but it is going to be more terrible for some. In denouncing the city of Capernaum for its refusal to believe in him, Jesus warned, "And you, Capernaum, will you be lifted to the heavens? No, you will go down to Hades. For if the miracles that were performed in you had been performed in Sodom, it would have remained to this day. But I tell you that it will be more bearable for Sodom on the Day of Judgment than for you."[12] Sodom was a depraved and wicked city which God destroyed by fire. This verse is not saying that the inhabitants

12 Matthew 11:23-24 (NIV)

of Sodom will be spared on judgment day. They will still be sentenced to the lake of fire, but it appears that they will suffer a lesser punishment than the people of Capernaum. James, the brother of the Lord Jesus and leader of the church in Jerusalem, said that teachers of the word of God would face a stricter judgment than other believers.[13] If this is true of the righteous, it will also be true of the unrighteous.

As previously stated, God is so holy that one sin in a person's life will be enough to see them cast into Gehenna, a place of separation, regret, and torment. But for some, their separation and anguish will be far greater. The justice of God demands that the perpetrators of atrocities against humanity will suffer a more fiery fate than others will.

However, no part of hell is going to be easy to bear. Jesus warned that there will be weeping and gnashing of teeth. I have sometimes heard people jest, "Well, my friends and I will end up in hell together; we'll just have a big party forever." This could not be further from the truth. In realising what they have lost, those who have rejected God will feel the utter pain accompanying the realisation that there is no second chance to be saved. This agony of being separated from God will not go away. It will be eternal and unrelenting.

Some may think that because they are good people, they will not end up in hell. The Bible actually says that there is none who are intrinsically good or righteous, not one.[14] "But cowards, unbelievers, the corrupt, murderers, the immoral, those who practice witchcraft, idol worshippers, and all liars," records the

---

13 See James 3:1
14 See Romans 3:10

apostle John, "their fate is in the fiery lake of burning sulphur. This is the second death."[15] Many may protest that they are not liars, murderers, idol worshippers, or immoral and are thus not deserving of hell. But notice the word *unbelievers* in that list (interpreted as faithless in some translations). If they refuse to believe in Jesus Christ and his offer of forgiveness, then that makes them an unbeliever. There is, therefore, no wiping away of their sins. Faithlessness can send a person to hell as much as murder can. The only righteousness that will spare people from hell is the righteousness of Christ gifted to them through faith.

False Theories of Hell

Because hell is so horrifying, it is hard for people to envisage that it is real. Many are happy to believe in a God of love and mercy, but the thought of a God of justice who will punish sin offends them. And it is not difficult to see why. The more we understand that God is a perfect Father who shows us unconditional love and mercy through Jesus, we may question, "Is there really going to be a hell that will last forever and will God actually send people there?" However, the Bible is very clear: God will punish those who have rebelled against him, and reward those who have obeyed him. Famed American pastor A. W. Tozer[16] warned, "The vague and tenuous hope that God is too kind to punish the ungodly has become a deadly opiate for the consciences of millions." Sentimentality and false notions about the love of God have led some Christians to embrace popular, but false, theories about hell.

---

15 Revelation 21:8
16 A.W. Tozer, 1897-1963

Here are three of the main ones:

1. Annihilationism

Because hell is called the second death, and because Jesus said that we should fear God who can destroy both body and soul in hell,[17] some believe that people cast into hell are exterminated; they simply cease to exist. The best interpreter of the Bible is itself, and we must look at these verses alongside others that clarify what this means. Speaking of the judgment of the nations, Jesus said, "Then the King will turn to those on the left and say, 'Away with you, you cursed ones, into the eternal fire prepared for the devil and his demons, ... and they will go away into eternal punishment, but the righteous will go into eternal life.'"[18] The word eternal means forever without end. Since we accept that the phrase 'eternal life' in this verse means never-ending bliss, why would we think that eternal fire and punishment is anything other than never-ending as well?

The apostle John describes those sentenced to hell, "They will be tormented with fire and burning sulphur in the presence of the holy angels and the Lamb. The smoke of their torment will rise forever and ever, and they will have no relief, day or night."[19] Speaking of Satan, John says, "Then the devil, who had deceived them, was thrown into the fiery lake of burning sulphur, joining the beast and the false prophet. There they will be tormented day and night forever and ever."[20] Hell was originally created for Satan and his angels when they revolted against God in heaven. When humankind also later rebelled,

---

17 See Matthew 10:28
18 Matthew 25: 41,46
19 Revelation 14:10b, 11a
20 Revelation 20:10

it became the final home of all who rebel against God's rule, including human beings. That is why Satan seeks to deceive multitudes into rejecting Christ so that he may drag as many as possible with him into the lake of fire. As much as we may like to believe in annihilationism, the Bible simply does not allow for it.

2. Universalism

This false belief declares that all will be saved, even if God gives them another chance after they die. I have observed many funerals for people who did not know God, yet the impression was given that they are in heaven, reunited with loved ones, and we all will join them one day. Sadly, this is not correct. Though God desires all to be saved,[21] not all will be. "Work hard to enter the narrow door to God's Kingdom," warned Jesus, "for many will try to enter but will fail. When the master of the house has locked the door, it will be too late. You will stand outside knocking and pleading, 'Lord, open the door for us!' But he will reply, 'I don't know you or where you come from.'"[22] While we may have a number of chances to receive Christ, they are confined to this life, for immediately after death comes a judgment to determine our destination. "Each person is destined to die once and after that comes judgment."[23]

3. Second Probationism

This erroneous belief teaches that a non-believer may get a second chance in Hades. Suffering in Hades is seen as a probationary period which, if responded to correctly, allows a person to enter heaven. In the story of the rich man and the

---

21 See 2 Peter 3:9, 1 Timothy 2:3-4

22 Luke 13:24-25

23 Hebrews 9:27

beggar, which we have already discussed, Jesus makes it clear that there is no second chance after death. "There is a great chasm separating us," says Abraham in the story. "No one can cross over to you from here [paradise], and *no one can cross over to us from there* [hell]."[24]

A mutated form of this error is the belief in Purgatory, an intermediate hell-like state (but not Hades or Gehenna) where, after death, a believer (but not a fully committed one) undergoes purification through suffering, so as to achieve the holiness necessary to enter heaven. Some people christened as babies,[25] but who have remained nominal Christians, hope that prayers offered by family or priests will see them bypass hell and get through Purgatory to heaven. There is no biblical precedent for such a false hope.

Belief in Purgatory infers that Christ's atoning death on the cross is not enough. Clearly this is wrong. "When God our Saviour revealed his kindness and love," writes the apostle Paul, "he saved us; not because of the righteous things we had done, but because of his mercy. He washed away our sins, giving us a new birth and new life through the Holy Spirit."[26] If we are saved on earth exclusively by God's grace and our faith in Christ, then why would it be necessary after death to endure a supposed Purgatory? God's grace is the same whether we are alive or dead. Belief in Purgatory confuses sanctification with

---

24 Luke 16:26 (emphasis mine)

25 Scripture teaches that water baptism is for those who have made a conscious decision to become a follower of Jesus. We are to first believe and then be baptised. See Mark 16:16.

26 Titus 3:4-5

justification.[27]

Hell Actually Showcases God's Love

Multitudes believe that there is no hell, and embrace any 'ism' that teaches this, or, as already stated, they simply believe that everyone goes to heaven. The Bible says one hundred and sixty-two times in the New Testament alone that hell exists. Some may feel Christians are callous proclaiming this, or ask how a God of love could create a horrific place like hell. Ironically, hell actually magnifies the mercy, goodness, and love of God. This is because God has gone to extreme lengths to ensure that no one has to go there: "For God so loved the world that he gave his one and only Son, that whoever believes in him shall not perish but have eternal life."[28] The words *so loved* indicate that, in giving up his son to redeem us from sin, death, and hell, God was motivated by great, great love for humankind. He wants all to have eternal life. He will take no pleasure in sending anyone to hell. If people live all their lives distancing themselves from God, then he will finally give them what they want. It is not God who sends people to hell, though he makes that final judgment; it is people who send themselves there. They will have made their choice, and God will be obliged by his justice to give them what they wanted. "Hell is the greatest compliment God has ever paid to the dignity of human freedom," wrote English author G.K. Chesterton.[29] How is God, the Father of all humanity, going to

---

27 Justification is being declared completely righteous by God through faith in Jesus Christ. Sanctification is the lifelong process of being made righteous so that our positional justification becomes an experiential reality.

28 John 3:16 (NIV)

29 G.K. Chesterton, 1874-1936

feel on Judgment Day? Might he be saying things like:

"Why didn't you believe?"

"Why didn't you see the evidence I put in the earth for my existence?"

"Why didn't you believe in my Son? He died so that you would not have to go to this place."

How sad that people will glimpse God's love for them too late. Astounded by his beautiful nature, they will long intensely to be in his presence. Yet, because sin cannot co-exist with the holy presence of God, he will be forced to eject them from his presence.

But What About Those Who Have Never Heard?

People may object, "What about those who have never heard of Jesus or the gospel? Surely God would be unfair to send them to hell?" God will not unfairly sentence anyone. He has provided three levels of revelation of his existence and thus opportunity to believe in him:

1. Creation.

"They know the truth about God," writes the apostle Paul, "because he has made it obvious to them. For ever since the world was created, people have seen the earth and sky. Through everything God made, they can clearly see his invisible qualities – his eternal power and divine nature. So they have no excuse for not knowing God."[30] The marvels of God's creation are not only for us to enjoy, but are given as signposts so that we may believe. Jon Comenius,[31] the father of modern education, termed creation *God's second book* after the Bible. The problem is that people start to foolishly worship creation instead of the creator. Paul continues, "They traded the truth about God for a lie. So they worshipped and served the things God created, instead of the Creator himself, who is worthy of eternal praise!"[32] Sadly, many look at creation and miss seeing God completely.

2. Conscience.

"Even Gentiles, who do not have God's written law, show that they know his law when they instinctively obey it," explains the Bible, "even without having heard it. They demonstrate that God's law is written in their hearts, for their own conscience and thoughts either accuse them or tell them they are doing right."[33] God writes his law on every human heart. People intrinsically know right from wrong. Unfortunately, the conscience can be seared and people can become hardened, dismissing sin's guilt and rejoicing in evil: "Everything is pure to those whose hearts are pure. But nothing is pure to those who are corrupt and unbelieving, because their minds and consciences are corrupted."[34]

3. Christ.

"Long ago God spoke many times and in many ways to our ancestors through the prophets," declares the Bible, "And now in these final days, he has spoken to us through his Son ... the

---

30 Romans 1:19-20
31 Jon Amos Comenius, 1592-1671
32 Romans 1:25
33 Romans 2:14-15
34 Titus 1:15

Son radiates God's own glory and expresses the very character of God, and he sustains everything by the mighty power of his command. When he had cleansed us from our sins, he sat down in the place of honour at the right hand of the majestic God in heaven."[35]

People are not saved by observing creation or following their consciences alone. Rather, creation and conscience allow them to have faith in God and it is that faith that saves them. How else could people under the Old Covenant be saved? They had faith in God and he gifted to them righteousness, even though, at the time, they had no clear revelation of Jesus the Messiah. "Abram believed the LORD," wrote Moses long before Christ appeared, "and he credited it to him as righteousness."[36] God actually backdated Christ's death on the cross to the believers of the Old Testament.

However, if creation and conscience are hints, then Christ is God's loudspeaker to reveal the way to him. He is the ultimate and clearest revelation of God's salvation. This is why he commanded his church to make him known to the ends of the earth. Thank God for his amazing grace shown in Jesus! He has come so that we would never have to face the terrible fate of hell. In the end we must trust that a perfectly holy and just God will judge fairly. The Bible asks rhetorically, "Shall not the Judge of all the earth do right [by executing just and righteous judgment]?"[37] He most certainly will. I believe that the Lord keeps drawing people to himself until the very end of their lives. Some keep resisting, but others may, in their final moments of

---

35 Hebrews 1: 1-3

36 Genesis 15:6 (NIV)

37 Genesis 18:25b (AMP)

life, yield to him. Only God can judge accurately.

Where Do We Stand?

Eternity is knocking, the clock is ticking, and the Day of Judgment will come. Where do you stand? Perhaps you have never given your life to Jesus, or perhaps you did once but are no longer walking with God and are far away from him. Salvation is the free gift of God - you cannot earn it. To be saved means you will not go to hell; you will spend eternity with God in a new heaven and new earth, and you will receive a glorious resurrection body. If a person was drowning and someone threw them a life preserver, they would grab it and say, "Thank you for saving me." Many people are drowning spiritually today because they do not know Jesus and thus they are headed for hell. You do not need to end up there. Jesus Christ died on a cross for you. If you believe in him and receive him, he will give you power to become a child of God. What Jesus did to keep us out of hell, and make sure that we would be with Him forever, is astounding.

The Bible says, "The "right time" is now. Today is the day of salvation."[38] Why delay? If you need to give your life to Christ, or if you have been away from him and need to come back to him, then I invite you to pray this simple prayer. As you mean it with all your being, God will answer you:

> Lord Jesus, please forgive all my sins. I don't want to be separated from you forever. Lord I want to be with you always. I believe you died for me, that you

[38] 2 Corinthians 6:2

> took the punishment for my sins so that I could be forgiven. Lord Jesus I turn from my sins and I receive you. I open the door of my life and ask you come in and take control. Lord, I give you my life. Amen.

If you prayed this prayer sincerely, then welcome to the family of God. May I suggest that you to do the following to help you grow in faith:

- Obtain a Bible and start reading it every day.

- Find a good Bible-believing church as soon as you are able, one that will encourage and strengthen you. Make friends with other keen Christians.

- Tell people what you have done. It is in telling others that you are a follower of Jesus Christ that your salvation is sealed: "If you openly declare that Jesus is Lord and believe in your heart that God raised him from the dead, you will be saved. For it is by believing in your heart that you are made right with God, and it is by openly declaring your faith that you are saved."[39]

- Keep enduring in your walk with God. Never waiver, despite the troubles of this life. It will be worth it in the end.

Judgment Day is not the end; rather it is the doorway to an even more wonderful event. We will examine this in the next chapter.

---

[39] Romans 10: 9-10

chapter fifteen

THE NEW HEAVEN AND EARTH

It was finally over. Thousands of years of misery, bloodshed and evil that had scarred the earth, were now at an end. God had judged the unrighteous and sentenced them to hell, along with Satan, the fallen angels, and demons. The righteous, in their glorified resurrection bodies, had been rewarded, and as the Bride of the Lamb,[1] been married to Christ. The old age had passed away. Now a new age could begin.

In a prophetic vision of that time, the apostle John wrote, "Then I saw a new heaven and a new earth, for the old heaven and the old earth had disappeared. And the sea was also gone."[2] Many centuries before, God had promised through the prophet Isaiah, "See, I will create new heavens and a new earth. The former things will not be remembered, nor will they come to

1 See Revelation 19:7
2 Revelation 21:1

mind."[3] A new earth, a pure atmosphere (the first heaven), and a fresh universe of stars and galaxies (the second heaven) will define the new age.

Might it be that the planets in our solar system and beyond, which are currently inhospitable to life, become habitable? Perhaps in the new earth technology will be so advanced that we will have the wonder of exploring them.

However, something even more amazing than these will characterise that era. The third heaven – God's home, the City of God, the heavenly Jerusalem[4] – will come down upon the earth. John continues, "And I saw the holy city, the new Jerusalem, coming down from God out of heaven like a bride beautifully dressed for her husband. I heard a loud shout from the throne, saying, "Look, God's home is now among his people! He will live with them, and they will be his people. God himself will be with them. He will wipe every tear from their eyes, and there will be no more death or sorrow or crying or pain. All these things are gone forever."[5] John goes onto say that the walls of the city were sixty-five metres thick and the city was pure gold, as clear as glass.[6]

Picture the scene: defying the law of gravity, the New Jerusalem will descend slowly from heaven – a massive, cubic

3 Isaiah 65:17 (NIV)
4 See Hebrews 12:22 for these names of heaven.
5 Revelation 21:2-4
6 See Revelation 21: 17-18

city measuring over two thousand kilometres[7] on all sides, the base as large as two-thirds the land mass of Australia, the top reaching into space. Made of gold as transparent as glass, and with walls and foundations of precious stones, the city will be the magnificent heart of the entire new earth. Its grandeur will be more than material however. The source of its glorious radiance will be God's splendour and presence. This will be the most perfect structure ever seen by the human eye. On a new earth without sea or ocean, the City of God will be the headquarters of a new universe. Thus, God's plan of restoration, outworked over millennia since the fateful day that Adam and Eve lost the paradise of Eden, and the earth fell under a curse, will be complete.

There is some debate as to whether the new earth will be a completely new creation or a restoration of the old earth. "But the day of the Lord will come as a thief in the night," writes the apostle Peter. "In which the heavens will pass away with a great noise, and the elements will melt with fervent heat; both the earth and the works that are in it will be burned up [laid bare]."[8] Some see the fire as purifying the old earth, which God will then re-establish. Others point to a later scripture, which describes this event as, "On that day, he will set the heavens on fire, and the elements will melt away in the flames."[9] That the elements (the basic building blocks of all matter) melt may point

---

7 Actually 2220 kilometers or 12000 stadia (12 X 1000). Some see these dimensions as symbolic of perfection, completion and government. Though such a huge city is beyond our current comprehension, nothing prevents the dimensions from being exact. To the people of John's day, a city with such unthinkably thick and high walls would be considered impregnable, and would have given them great comfort and security.

8 2 Peter 3:10 (NKJV)

9 2 Peter 3:12b

to a total destruction of the old, and the creation of a brand new earth and heavens. Whether God restores or re-creates the earth, it will be vastly superior to the current one.

There will be no sea, but this does not prevent there being fresh water lakes and rivers. Today's Dead Sea is dead because of its high salt content, and normal seawater is undrinkable, so it is possible that there will simply be no salty water in the new earth, which will be a place of perfect life.

Further, the new earth will be so beautiful, that no-one will remember, or even give a thought to, the old one any more. The previous world and its evils will be gone forever. The curse of pain, toil, death and decay that brought such sorrow, will have passed away; creation's groan will have ended. Never again will there be any suffering, distress, sickness, or death. The Lord will have vanquished sin and death forever. The apostle Peter voices all our hopes when he says, "But we are looking forward to the new heavens and new earth he has promised, a world filled with God's righteousness."[10]

A Source of Hope

What the apostles Peter and John saw, has proven a source of hope for all generations of believers, especially in times of adversity. Others have seen this New Jerusalem, too. Many who have died and been resuscitated have claimed to have had out-of-body experiences. A number describe visiting heaven and seeing a city with various levels, streets of gold as clear as crystal, and many beautiful mansions, similar to John's description.

---

10 2 Peter 3:13

Listen to the account of one cardiac arrest victim:

> Immediately my spirit left my body, I saw the City of the Great King … I was looking down on the most dazzling sight imaginable. All the adjectives one could use – beautiful, splendid, picturesque, colourful, magnificent – are totally inadequate to describe this place … there were three levels in that city and seemingly millions of miles of streets; avenues of solid gold, not paved with gold but solid and yet, at the same time, transparent. It was the purest, cleanest and brightest gold imaginable, and looked like ribbons of magnifying glass. Everywhere, through the streets and as far as I could see, were millions of mansions.[11]

See chapter ten for a wider description of the city, including vegetation, rivers, animal life and so on. The righteous will not spend eternity in a never-ending church service sitting on heavenly clouds playing harps! This glorious heavenly city will come to earth, and God will live with his people. God will fully manifest his Kingdom – with its King – universally and physically on earth. It is the ultimate act of a loving God, to bring his home, heaven, to our home, earth, and for God and his people to be one forever. What are some of the features of the New Jerusalem and the new earth itself?

---

11 Richard Kent & Val Fotherby, *The Final Frontier*, London, Marshall Pickering, 1997, p.71.

No Night

Like the holiest place where God dwelt in the temple of the Old Covenant, the city itself is a perfect cube. And its gates are always open. In other words, there is direct access to the presence of God. "I saw no temple in the city," writes John, "for the Lord God Almighty and the Lamb are its temple. And the city has no need of sun or moon, for the glory of God illuminates the city, and the Lamb is its light.[12] Darkness never invades this city; the Lord bathes it in constant daylight. "Its gates will never be closed at the end of the day because there is no night there"[13] and "the nations will walk by its light, and the kings of the earth will bring their splendour into it."[14] This city is the manifestation of God; so radiant with his presence, that it will light the whole of the new earth. Perpetual daylight infers that people may not need sleep in their resurrection bodies.

Organic Paradise

"Then the angel showed me a river with the water of life, clear as crystal, flowing from the throne of God and of the Lamb. It flowed down the centre of the main street. On each side of the river grew a tree of life, bearing twelve crops of fruit, with a fresh crop each month. The leaves were used for medicine to heal the nations. No longer will there be a curse upon anything."[15]

---

12 Revelation 21: 22-23
13 Revelation 21: 25
14 Revelation 21: 24 (NIV)
15 Revelation 22: 1-3a

Elements of the Garden of Eden are present in the city. As there was a great river in Eden,[16] so also a mighty river flows through the city. The main street is the heart and centre of any city and it is precisely here that the river flows. Because its source is the throne of God, the river contains the crystal-clear water of life. Everything about the city is pure, clear, and transparent. On each bank grows a tree of life, nourished by the life-giving waters, yielding twelve crops of fruit to bring healing and everlasting life.

Monthly crops – something that is unheard of in this present world – speak of incredible fertility in the new earth. We will drink from the river of life, eat fruit from the tree of life, and live forever. Leaves for healing probably refers to God healing the nations of this current earth from the curse, as in our resurrection bodies we will never become sick.

The term *monthly* may be a figurative way of saying continuously, or if literal, as is most likely, might mean that time does not cease in the new earth. While eternity is everlasting, and God is outside of time, living in the eternal present,[17] time is God's gift to humankind, and with the curse lifted, may become a benevolent servant to us, rather than the harsh taskmaster it is today. Perhaps we will be aware of time passing, but overjoyed that it will never run out. Time will tell! John Newton may have got it right when he wrote, "When we've been there ten thousand years, bright shining as the sun; we've no less days to sing God's praise than when we'd first begun."[18]

---

16 See Genesis 2:10

17 One day with God is like a thousand years and a thousand years is like a day. See 2 Peter 3:8

18 John Newton, 1725-1807. Words from the hymn *Amazing Grace*.

In Eden, there were also two special trees. One was the tree of life, the other the tree of the knowledge of good and evil. This latter tree, through which death came, and symbolising free will, is absent in the city. Jesus Christ, the Lamb of God, has forever paid for sin and broken the power of the evil nature in humanity. In their resurrection bodies, the saints are like Christ, and never again will there be any potential to sin. In the New Jerusalem, the tree of life grows on both sides of the riverbank. In other words, in place of what proved to be a tree of death, there is a second tree of life. The curse of sin and death is completely broken!

No doubt, the wider earth outside the city will be at least as luxuriant and beautiful as Eden was and probably more so. If God's first creation was very good, then his new creation will be even more glorious. John mentions nations and kings bringing their glory into the city. This could refer to the righteous nations and rulers of the old earth, but it more likely suggests that nations of redeemed, glorified people will inhabit the new earth, with the city as a focal point of worship and central government. With the whole earth a single, huge, borderless landmass, there will be no geographic isolation. Rather there will be complete unity and perfect love.

Peace

Isaiah the prophet predicted, "The LORD will mediate between nations and will settle international disputes. They will hammer their swords into plowshares and their spears into pruning hooks. Nation will no longer fight against nation, nor train for war anymore."[19] Premillennialists see this being fulfilled in a literal thousand-year reign of Christ on earth prior to the new earth, while others see it eventually happening on the current earth as God's Kingdom is advanced by the church (postmillennial view) or in the new earth (amillennial view). Whatever view believers may have, they can all agree that it will also be a feature of the new earth.

People today are desperate for peace; they are sick of war, violence, and terrorism. The world currently spends trillions of dollars on armaments. Nations have to have armies, navies, and air forces to protect their borders, because this current world is so hostile. However, in that day there will be no hostility and no need to produce arms. There will be economic abundance for all because the earth's resources will be employed in a constructive, rather than destructive way.

Peace will define the created order as well, the curse having been broken off the earth. The Bible predicts, "In that day the wolf and the lamb will live together; the leopard will lie down with the baby goat. The calf and the yearling will be safe with the lion, and a little child will lead them all. The cow will graze near the bear. The cub and the calf will lie down together. The lion will eat hay like a cow. Nothing will hurt or destroy in all my holy mountain, for as the waters fill the sea, so the earth will be filled with people who know the Lord."[20] Because these verses mention a child (there will be no children in the new earth), some see this prophecy as being fulfilled in the current earth, or others in the millennial reign of Christ. However, this zoological harmony will also be a feature of the eternal new earth.

---

19 Isaiah 2:4

20 Isaiah 11:6-7, 9

The animal kingdom is very brutal today. If the wolf and the lamb tried to lie down together, the lamb would be dinner! In the original creation, humans and animals alike were vegetarian and were at peace with one another. The Bible records God as saying to humankind, "Look! I have given you every seed-bearing plant throughout the earth and all the fruit trees for your food. And I have given every green plant as food for all the wild animals, the birds in the sky, and the small animals that scurry along the ground – everything that has life."[21] However, because of the fall into sin, the whole world order changed. God will restore that original order again.

He will not leave the plant kingdom out of this restoration either. "Where once there were thorns," predicts Isaiah the prophet, "cypress trees will grow. Where nettles grew, myrtles will sprout up."[22] Nothing in the entire plant kingdom will be termed a weed, or considered harmful, or a nuisance in the new earth. Everything will be beautiful and useful. I imagine that the earth will be one huge, luxuriant garden with verdant plains, majestic forests, and crystal-clear lakes and rivers.

One Language

The Bible predicts that God will one day restore a universal language: "I will purify the lips of the peoples, that all of them may call on the name of the LORD and serve him shoulder to shoulder."[23] Some see this as referring to the preaching of the one message of the gospel in New Testament times, while others see it fulfilled in the outpouring of the gift of tongues

---

21 Genesis 1:29, 30
22 Isaiah 55:13
23 Zephaniah 3:9 (NIV)

on Pentecost Day. There is nothing, however, to stop this verse being literal. "At one time," records Moses, "all the people of the world spoke the same language and used the same words."[24] God gifted this language to Adam and Eve so that they could communicate with him and each other. Due to having a common speech, the human race was completely one. In pride, however, it attempted to build a city with a tower that would reach into heaven. God judged the peoples and confused their languages, causing the one race to separate into distinct nations.[25]

The new earth will see a full reversal of this judgment. The saints will once again have a common language – possibly a restoration of the ancient language Adam and Eve spoke – and this will contribute to the complete unity we will enjoy. The restoration of Jews from all over the world to their homeland of Israel, in our day, is a forerunner of this. It has necessitated the reviving of the Hebrew language, once considered dead, so that the people could have a common language. This has helped to make Israel a strong nation.

The Ultimate

I believe that technology, art, music, and many other facets of creation will be present in the new earth. God will not return us to some primitive, agrarian state. He has placed secrets in his creation that will unfold to us as never before. There will be both work and worship: "For the throne of God and of the Lamb will be there, and his servants will worship him."[26] Servants mean there will be service. Those permitted to be part of the new

---

24 Genesis 11:1

25 See Genesis 11: 2-9

26 Revelation 22:3b

world, who have believed in the Son, will both serve God with purposeful tasks in eternity and worship him with adoration, for "they will see his face, and his name will be written on their foreheads."[27]

That is the ultimate wonder of the City of God: seeing God's face. "For now we see only a reflection as in a mirror; then we shall see face to face."[28] Face to face. It is the privilege Adam and Eve had but then lost. It has been the longing of God's people throughout history. King David distilled this hope when he sang, "I will see you. When I awake, I will see you face to face and be satisfied."[29] Full satisfaction for the human soul will come only with the privilege of seeing God face to face. It is a pleasure that believers in heaven now enjoy, and a pleasure all believers will enjoy in the new earth. It is what we were made for.

All praise to Jesus who made it possible – that on the cross he shed his blood for our sin. If he had not, then the City of God would remain in heaven, forever beyond the reach of men and women. "For you know that God paid a ransom to save you from the empty life inherited from your ancestors," marvelled the apostle Peter, "And it was not paid with mere gold or silver. It was the precious blood of Christ, the sinless, spotless Lamb of God. God chose him as your ransom long before the world began, but now in these last days he has been revealed for your sake."[30]

What gratitude this should inspire in us! What a privilege to

---

27 Revelation 22:4
28 1 Corinthians 13:12 (NIV)
29 Psalm 17:15
30 1 Peter 1:18-20

tell others about this wonderful good news! This truly is amazing grace. "For the sin of this one man, Adam, caused death to rule over many. But even greater is God's wonderful grace and his gift of righteousness, for all who receive it will live in triumph over sin and death through this one man, Jesus Christ."[31]

The Second Adam and Eve

Jesus died not only to bring us to the Father; but also to bring the Father to us. In the new earth, Christ will present the church to the Father as his family. Likewise, the Father will present the church to the Son as his Bride. We will be forever married to Christ, the Lamb of God. The city of redeemed people made faultless is, said John, "the bride, the wife of the Lamb."[32] This speaks of love and perfect relationship. Think of it: Christ, the second Adam,[33] will stand with his bride, the second Eve, in a new creation! What the first Adam and Eve failed to do in ruling the earth in righteousness, the second Adam and Eve will achieve. Who knows what purposes will unfold as Christ and his Bride rule a new universe for eternity, under the Father's approving smile? That is worth living for and holding on in faith to receive.

God revealed these things not so that we would be escapists fantasising about a future world, while we take a cruise ship to eternity, but so that we could live with purpose and unshakeable hope throughout this present life. True hope reaches into eternity and glimpses what is coming. "And if our hope in Christ is only

---

31 Romans 5: 17

32 Revelation 21: 9

33 See 1 Corinthians 15:45

for this life," said Paul, "we are more to be pitied than anyone in the world."[34] It is fine to have hopes and dreams for this life, but if they end there, what good is that? Rather, it is also the hope of what is to come – reigning with Christ in a new heaven and earth where there will be no sickness or sin or poverty or war or death – a hope that reaches into eternity, beyond this life, beyond the grave. It is the hope of a world restored to God, the Kingdom of God manifest in all its glory, and of the resurrection of the dead.

We are pilgrims on a journey from a garden we lost, to a city we will gain – children of Abraham, the pilgrim father of faith. He was content to live in a tent all his life because, as the book of Hebrews says, "Abraham was confidently looking forward to a city with eternal foundations, a city designed and built by God."[35] Like Abraham, we can say with God's people through the ages, "For this world is not our permanent home; we are looking forward to a home yet to come."[36] When we glimpse the City of God, the New Jerusalem, the consummation of God's plan of the ages, it will change the way we live. The apostle Paul saw it and declared, "So I run with purpose in every step."[37] Paul journeyed well, and so should we.

In the final chapter, we will discuss how to do this.

---

34 1 Corinthians 15: 19
35 Hebrews 11: 10
36 Hebrews 13:14
37 1 Corinthians 9:26a

chapter sixteen

A FINAL WORD

Heaven and the afterlife can be difficult concepts to grasp for rationalists who believe only in a material universe. To them there is no spiritual realm, or eternal spirit within a person. While Christians honour the created, material world, they also know, by revelation from the Bible, and the inner witness of the Holy Spirit, that the spiritual realm is very real. Rationalists believe that, at death, a person ceases to exist, that in the future our sun will vaporise the earth, and the universe will explode or implode into nothingness. How wrong they are. Such a view is fatalistic and gives no hope.

Christians also understand that one day there will be a far superior material creation – the new earth and heavens. There, our redeemed spirits, clothed in glorious resurrection bodies, will enjoy a new and everlasting existence. This gives believers great comfort when mourning the loss of loved ones. Death is not forever; rather it is a beginning. Around 125 A.D., a perplexed Greek by the name of Aristeides wrote to one of his friends, trying to explain the extraordinary success of the new

Christian religion. In his letter he said, "If any righteous man among the Christians passes from this world, they rejoice and offer thanks to God, and they accompany his body with songs and thanksgiving, as if he was going from one place to another nearby!"[1]

King Solomon, the wisest man who ever lived, declared, "The day you die is better than the day you are born."[2] As we have seen, believers should look forward to the day of their death. Solomon added, "A wise person thinks a lot about death, while a fool thinks only about having a good time."[3] This does not mean that we should have a morbid fascination with death; rather we should soberly remind ourselves that death will one day come calling. And when it does, God wants us to be ready for it, and the world to come.

A Warning

Some time ago, while staying in Bristol, England, the Holy Spirit gave me a very clear vision. I saw the most vivid expanse of deep, deep orange. Jesus, clothed in the purest white robe, stood in the midst of it and said to me, "The sun is setting on history, and I am coming soon." Inquisitively, I asked about all the theories concerning the events connected to his return, to which he smiled and replied, "My people have been trying to precisely determine those events for two thousand years." Jesus then quoted the scripture, "Many are the plans in a person's

---

1 www.sermonillustrations.com/a-z/d/death.htm. Accessed 17/12/15.
2 Ecclesiastes 7:1b
3 Ecclesiastes 7:4

heart, but it is the LORD's purpose that prevails,"[4] and said that it would be that way with his return. In other words, we won't be able to figure it out fully until it happens.

He added that his followers should observe the signs of the times but not obsess about them. Rather, we are to live our lives wisely, purposefully, and with urgency, during our time on earth. To obsess over signs and events is like a person who is so preoccupied with weather forecasts that they never go outside to experience the day. Jesus concluded with a sombre warning, "My coming will be a great and terrible day. It will be great because prior to it, there will be a widespread move of my Spirit that will see multitudes saved, as my Father is not wanting any to perish. It will be terrifying for those who reject this offer of salvation. Pray for the harvest rains to come and deluge the earth, and for labourers to reap the harvest."

If you are not yet a committed follower of the Lord Jesus Christ, I urge you to become one. This is no fairy tale. What I have written in this book is the truth, according to the Bible. Jesus is the only way to eternal life. "Salvation is found in no one else," declared the apostle Peter emphatically, "for there is no other name under heaven given to mankind by which we must be saved."[5] In his mercy, God the Father "wants everyone to be saved and to understand the truth."[6] By believing in his son and receiving Jesus into your life, you will become a child of God.

If you are already a follower of Jesus, let a passion to live for him grip you and inspire you to help others find salvation

---

4 See Proverbs 19:21
5 Acts 4:12 (NIV)
6 1 Timothy 2:4

in him, so that they too may enter the new earth. "For I am not ashamed of the gospel, because it is the power of God that brings salvation to everyone who believes: first to the Jew, then to the Gentile."[7] In Paul's day, Jews were those close to God, and Gentiles were those far away from him.

There may be people in your life – family members, friends, neighbours, colleagues – who are near to salvation or who are far away from God. Whatever their state, the gospel is the power of God for salvation! Evangelist Reinhard Bonnke has said, "A gospel that is not shared is no gospel at all." The truth about heaven, hell, and the new earth compels us to share it, teach it, speak it, and live it out.

"I am sending you to the Gentiles," explained Jesus to the apostle Paul, "to open their eyes, so they may turn from darkness to light and from the power of Satan to God. Then they will receive forgiveness for their sins and be given a place among God's people, who are set apart by faith in me."[8]

Can you hear Jesus' longing for lost souls in those words? That is why he sends his church. The apostle Paul is not here anymore; today it is us. We are the current generation to whom Jesus says, "I am sending you." To do what? To turn people from darkness to light. He wants them to receive a place, not in hell but in the new heaven and the new earth.

---

7 Romans 1:16 (NIV)
8 Acts 26:17b-18

The Power of Prayer

As we catch God's heart for lost people, may his love compel us to reach out to them and also to pray.

Satan blinds many with his lies, making it difficult for them to see the light of the truth. Prayer, however, can overcome this as long as we are persistent. George Müller[9] was a renowned Christian philanthropist and preacher in Victorian England, who cared for over ten thousand orphans through his orphanages in Bristol. He also established numerous schools that educated more than one hundred thousand children.

One time, he became concerned for five of his non-believing friends. So he began to pray for them. After some months, one of them came to the Lord. Ten years later, two others were converted. It took twenty-five years before the fourth man was saved. Müller persevered in prayer another twenty-seven years for the fifth friend, and throughout those five decades never gave up hope that he would accept Christ. Then Müller died. God rewarded his faith however, for soon after the funeral the last friend surrendered his life to Christ.[10]

Here is the point: there are some people in your life who may come to Christ quickly. Others may take years or even decades. And some you may not see saved in your lifetime – but you will see it from heaven.

Never give up. Never stop loving, never stop believing, and

---

9 George Müller 1805-1898

10 www.sermonillustrations.com/a-z/p/perseverance.htm. Accessed 20/12/14

never stop praying. "The earnest prayer of a righteous person," declares the Bible, "has great power and produces wonderful results."[11] Prayer alone may not save someone; they also need to hear the message of the gospel. However, prayer can be a powerful catalyst for them to receive Christ.

In a church that Greta and I once ministered in, an elderly woman shared the following story with us: "I prayed for my husband for forty-three years and, two weeks before he died, he came to Christ. I prayed for my backslidden son for twenty-seven years, and one day out of the blue, he told me that he needed God!"

Do not give up, for this is a matter of life and death, heaven and hell. It is a matter of whether people go to the lake of fire or enter the new heaven and earth.

Our Longing

For such a small epistle, the book of 1 Thessalonians has eleven references to the return of Jesus Christ and the resurrection from the dead. This theme pulsates from the pages of every chapter. The apostle Paul wrote it to encourage those new converts in Thessalonica that they should not grieve bitterly over fellow Christians who had died, and to reassure them that one day they would rise from the dead and be reunited with them. Consider the first and last of these references, which form eschatological bookends within the epistle:

"They [other believers] speak of how you are looking forward

---

11 James 5:16b

to the coming of God's Son from heaven – Jesus, whom God raised from the dead. He is the one who has rescued us from the terrors of the coming judgment."[12]

"May God himself, the God of peace, sanctify you through and through. May your whole spirit, soul and body, be kept blameless at the coming of our Lord Jesus Christ. The one who calls you is faithful, and he will do it."[13]

This is still a message for us today. Like the Thessalonians of old, may we long for the return of Jesus to rule the earth, and be grateful that we will not have to face the terrors of Judgment Day. And, like Paul, may we have confidence that God's faithfulness and power is able to keep us strong and blameless until that day.

Some of the topics we have discussed concerning life after death, may seem a little confusing at first glance. Yet the Bible says that this should be basic knowledge for every believer, just as it was to the Thessalonians. "Therefore, leaving the discussion of the elementary principles of Christ, let us go on to perfection," instructs the word of God, "not laying again the foundation of repentance from dead works and of faith toward God, of the doctrine of baptisms, of laying on of hands, of resurrection of the dead, and of eternal judgment."[14] If these truths are etched into our lives, then we will grasp that "our citizenship is in heaven, from which we also eagerly wait for the Saviour, the Lord Jesus Christ"[15] and nothing in this world will be able to

---

12 1 Thessalonians 1:10

13 1 Thessalonians 5:23-24 (NIV)

14 Hebrews 6: 1-2 (NKJV)

15 Philippians 3:20 (NKJV)

rob us from that hope. This will also keep us from living like this world is all there is.

My prayer is that this book will have comforted you if you have lost loved ones, encouraged you to run your spiritual race with endurance to the end, and awakened an urgency to see unsaved people come to Christ. I pray that it may also have compelled you to give your life to Christ if you have not done so already.

Writing *Afterlife* has been a wonderful journey for Greta and me. To write part one, *Life after Death for the Living*, we reread our journals to get a renewed feel for the events surrounding the deaths of Jane and Ron. Fresh tears resulted as we relived the losses we had suffered, mixed with tears of appreciation for what God had done in healing us and bringing us together.

In writing part two, *Life after Death for the Departed*, I became overawed with the magnitude of God's love in rescuing us from the judgment to come. It drew me closer to Jesus and the Father more than ever before. I pray that it will be the same for you.

The words of the song *You are Beautiful*[16] say it well:

I see You there hanging on a tree
You bled and then you died and then you rose again for me
Now You are sitting on Your heavenly throne
Soon we will be coming home
You're beautiful!

When we arrive at eternity's shore
Where death is just a memory and tears are no more
We'll enter in as the wedding bells ring
Your bride will come together and we'll sing
You're beautiful!

Perhaps it is best to leave the final words of this book to an angel. God sent him to the prophet Daniel to explain puzzling visions of the last days that the Holy Spirit had given him. Even after the angel's explanations, Daniel commented, "I heard what he said, but I did not understand what he meant. So I asked, 'How will all this finally end, my lord?'"[17] After stating that the full understanding would be kept secret until the time of the end, the angel simply said to Daniel, "As for you, go your way until the end. You will rest, and then at the end of the days, you will rise again to receive the inheritance set aside for you."[18]

And what the angel said to Daniel is what God says to us.

16 Phil Wickham, "You are Beautiful," ©2007, from the album *Cannons*.
17 Daniel 12:8
18 Daniel 12:13

Hope

In today's world, so many live with disappointment – never daring to dream or to have hope. In life, we all eventually encounter trouble. However, God promises "I will transform the valley of trouble into a gateway of hope." In every valley of trouble or disappointment, there is a doorway of hope waiting to be found.

What lies beyond the doorway? Purpose. A shift from hope deferred, to God-given desires fulfilled. A glimpse of the age to come. This book will help you discover that doorway. If you have lost hope, or want to develop a rugged, confident, biblical hope that is more than mere wishful thinking, then this book is for you.

"Full of gripping personal stories that made me weep and worship. I was encouraged and instructed by the great wisdom set down in these pages."
– *John Dawson, President, Youth With A Mission*

LifeWords

High quality 16 GB USB drive that contains all 18 audio and 16 video messages available from SpiritLife Ministries in mp3 and mp4 format. Play on your computer, smart TV, or any car or stereo with a USB input. A great resource for churches and individuals. Comes in a display case.

These additional resources can be purchased from the authors on their website: www.spiritlife.org.nz

ABOUT THE AUTHORS

After graduating from Canterbury University, Christchurch, New Zealand, with a B.Sc. (Hons) degree in Chemistry, David became a secondary school teacher and soon after pastored Elim churches in Picton and Wellington, together with his first wife Jane. He subsequently joined the pastoral staff of Auckland City Elim Church, but resigned three years later to become caregiver for Jane who had become disabled with multiple sclerosis. In 2003 he and Jane commenced an itinerant prophetic / teaching ministry within New Zealand. Jane passed away in 2007. David later married Greta, and they have five sons between them.

After completing her B.Sc. (Physiotherapy) at the University of Cape Town, South Africa, Greta worked for some years at Groote Schuur Hospital before doing a post graduate Diploma in Teaching Physiotherapy. She lectured at UCT until the birth of her two sons. Early in their marriage, she and her first husband Ron studied extramurally with the Theological College of South Africa and were involved in youth ministry at the Assemblies of God Churches in Cape Town. Greta also worked in children's ministry for many years.

In 1997 the family immigrated to Auckland, New Zealand where Ron passed away in early 2008. Greta ran her physiotherapy practice until late 2008 when she married David. Together with David, she helped found SpiritLife Ministries, and exercises a strong prophetic ministry in their travels.

David and Greta are currently based at Church Unlimited, a large, multicultural church in Auckland. They travel extensively both within New Zealand and overseas, inspiring people to have unwavering hope despite life's circumstances and equipping them to operate in the supernatural power of the Holy Spirit in daily life.

To contact the authors, write to:

David and Greta Peters
P.O Box 69012, Glendene,
Auckland 0645, New Zealand

Email: davidp@spiritlife.org.nz

Website: www.spiritlife.org,nz